# Spiritual Maturity: The Normal Christian Life

# Spiritual Maturity: The Normal Christian Life

*Donna L. Preston*

© 2018 Donna L. Preston
All rights reserved.

ISBN-13: 9781983938832
ISBN-10: 1983938831

# Table Of Contents

Chapter 1 Foundation for Spiritual Advancement. . . . . . . . . . . . . . . 1
             Scriptures on Seeking · · · · · · · · · · · · · · · · · · · · · · · · 4
             An Ancient Greek Man Who Searched: "For the
             Reason of things" · · · · · · · · · · · · · · · · · · · · · · · · · · · · 5
             Jesus, Paul and Believers: A Brief Comparison · · · · · · · 6
             Reverend John Wesley (From two sermons) · · · · · · · · · · 9
                  The Young Minister · · · · · · · · · · · · · · · · · · · · · · · · 9
                  The Elder Statesman, Founder of Methodism · · · · · · · · 9
             An Open Letter to Evangelicals · · · · · · · · · · · · · · · · · ·11
             Reflections on Studying the New Testament · · · · · · · · ·13
Chapter 2 <u>The Gospel of John: The Holy Spirit</u> · · · · · · · · · · · · · ·15
             Hearing and doing are imperative to believing.
Chapter 3 <u>The Acts of the Apostle</u> · · · · · · · · · · · · · · · · · · · · · · ·24
             Honorable people · · · · · · · · · · · · · · · · · · · · · · · · · · · · ·24
             One Scripture clarifies another. · · · · · · · · · · · · · · · · · · · 26
Chapter 4 <u>Paul's Epistle to the Romans, Chapters 1 and 2</u> · · · · · · · · ·31
             "Believe by the things that are made."
             His judgment is against unrighteousness.
             <u>Paul's Epistle to the Romans, Chapters 3 and 4</u> · · · · · · · ·37
             "Not of works" refers to the Jewish Law.
             <u>Paul's Epistle to the Romans, Chapter 4</u> · · · · · · · · · · · · ·45
             Abraham's obedience imputed him, "a righteous man."

Paul's Epistle to the Romans, Chapter 5 · · · · · · · · · · · · · ·51
"He bore our sins; therefore we should live unto righteousness."
Paul's Epistle to the Romans, Chapter 6 · · · · · · · · · · · · · ·53
"Yield to God as instruments of righteousness."
Paul's Epistle to the Romans, Chapter 7 · · · · · · · · · · · · · ·56
How to overcome sin, perplexed him.
Paul's Epistle to the Romans, Chapter 8 · · · · · · · · · · · · · ·58
"Those guided by the Spirit are the sons of God."
Paul's Epistle to the Romans, Chapters 9 and 10 · · · · · · · · · 62
To his brethren, "Seek righteousness by faith. Faith comes by hearing."
Paul's Epistle to the Romans, Chapter 11 · · · · · · · · · · · · 66
Parable of the wild olive tree.
Paul's Epistle to the Romans, Chapters 12-16 (A Brief Overview) · · · · · · · · · · · · · · · · · · · · · · · · · 68
The importance of goodness and keeping the Commandments.
Love defined as, "working no ill toward others."

Chapter 5 Paul's First Epistle to the Corinthians · · · · · · · · · · · · · · · ·71
Our responsibility in Spiritual growth.
The Spiritual Life
Paul's Second Epistle to the Corinthians · · · · · · · · · · · ·75
Our responsibility in Spiritual growth.
The Spiritual Life
Paul's Epistle to the Ephesians · · · · · · · · · · · · · · · · · · · · · 79
A poignant correspondence to the Gentile-Christians.
Paul's First Epistle to Timothy · · · · · · · · · · · · · · · · · · · 82
"Be an example to believers."
Paul's Epistle to the Hebrews · · · · · · · · · · · · · · · · · · · · · · 84
The Provocation.

Chapter 6 The Epistle of James · · · · · · · · · · · · · · · · · · · · · · · · · · 88
"Be doers of the word, not hearers only."

The Second Epistle of Peter · · · · · · · · · · · · · · · · · · · · · · · · 91
*Righteousness:* "Be diligent to be found blameless."
The First Epistle of John, Chapters 1-4 · · · · · · · · · · · · · 95
"He that says he abides in Him, ought to walk as
He walked."
The First Epistle of John, Chapter 5 · · · · · · · · · · · · · · · · 96
Scriptures that augment believing.
The Second and Third Epistles of John · · · · · · · · · · · · 98
The 'walk' and the 'good.'
Chapter 7 Biographical · · · · · · · · · · · · · · · · · · · · · · · · · · · · · · · 99

Bibliography · · · · · · · · · · · · · · · · · · · · · · · · · · · · · · · · · · · · 121

CHAPTER 1

# Foundation for Spiritual Advancement

THE INCLINATION FOR SPIRITUAL GROWTH is not unusual among Christians, however most people do not know how to begin, or the course to take. A silent desperation might prevail for those who have cherished the thought of "striving for the mastery," except ordinary sermons are the norm, and they cannot conceive of there being accomplished souls in our time such as St. Augustine or Fox to provide an example, or assist them in some manner. On asking clergy how to have more of the Holy Spirit, the reply may be, "When you accepted Jesus as your Savior, you were given the Holy Spirit."

There are certain basic truths that must be assimilated and followed in any area of higher learning, and striving for a higher quality of life equals the best in requirements or pre-conditions. "Those who worship Him must worship in Spirit and in Truth." Truth requires the active intellect. Believers should pause for a time from singing songs of confidence-in-eternal-security such as, "I know that all is well with my soul." Set aside the hearing or speaking of long, solicitous prayers, and study the New Testament, Psalms and Proverbs with the intent of determining, "what are my responsibilities?" People may need to be purged of a considerable amount of information previously taught, that may have a restraining influence regarding their standing before God. The hope lies in the fact that when one is on the right course, they will intuitively know it.

To "walk worthy of the Lord," is foundational to advancing. The satisfaction in succeeding at any cause applies especially to the "walk in newness of life," whereby a person is "growing in favor with God and man." The Apostle Paul's designation: "Let him become a new creature."

This ultimate transition has the obvious benefit of faith increasing. <u>Clement of Alexandria</u>, the teacher in the earliest Christian school wrote, "Faith grows with the exercise of obedience, and becomes a kind of Divine mutual and reciprocal correspondence."

New insight comes in the form of correction and guidance, and along the way dawns the recognition of the Spiritual presence urging one along to a loftier standing in all aspects of life.

There is nothing like becoming alert to the prompting of the Holy Spirit in the interests of the transformation. A problem or a flaw comes to mind, and we can either dismiss it as a passing thought, or consider it crucial to work through should Spiritual growth continue.

<u>Ralph W. Emerson, in his 1838 "Divinity School Address," spoke in part:</u>
"The divine bards are the friends of my intellect. They admonish me that the gleams which flash across my mind are not mine, but are of God. That they had the like, and were not disobedient to the Heavenly vision. Noble provocations go out from them inviting me to resist evil, to subdue evil and to be, and thus by His holy thoughts, Jesus serves us, and thus only.

To aim to convert a person by miracles is a profanation of the soul... Only by coming again to themselves, or to God in themselves, can they grow forevermore. It is a low benefit to give me something. It is a high benefit to enable me to do somewhat of myself.

The time is coming when all men will see that the gift of God to the soul is not a vaunting, overpowering, excluding sanctity, but a sweet, natural goodness. A goodness like thine and mine, and that invites thine and mine to be and to grow."

<u>Thomas a' Kempis, "The Imitation of Christ:"</u>
"Christ will come unto thee, and show thee His consolations, if thou prepare for Him a worthy mansion within thee."

# SCRIPTURES ON SEEKING
## The Old Testament

**1 Chronicles 28-9** "The Lord searches all hearts, and understands all the imaginations of the thoughts. If thou seek Him, He will be found of thee."
**2 Chronicles 19-3** "Nevertheless there are good things found in thee. Thou hast prepared thy heart to seek God."
**2 Chronicles 30-19** "Hezekiah prayed for them saying, 'The good Lord pardon everyone that prepares his heart to seek God.'"
**Deuteronomy 4-29** "If thou seek the Lord thy God, thou shall find Him if thou seek Him with all thy heart and with all thy soul."
**Zephaniah 2-3** "Seek you the Lord all you gentle of the earth. Seek righteousness, that it may be you shall be hid in the day of the Lord's anger."
**Book of Job 8-5** "If thou would seek unto God betimes, and make thy supplication to the Almighty; if thou were pure and upright, surely now He would awaken for thee."

## The New Testament
**The Gospel of Luke 12-31** "Seek you first the Kingdom of God, and all these things will be added unto you."
**The Acts of the Apostles 17-27, 28** ..."That they should seek the Lord, if haply they might find Him, though He is not far from every one of us."
**Paul's Epistle to the Hebrews 11-6** "He is a rewarder of those who diligently seek Him."
**The Epistle of James 4-8** "Draw nigh to God, and He will draw nigh to you."

# AN ANCIENT GREEK MAN WHO SEARCHED
"For the reason of things."

<u>Xenophanes</u> 536 B.C. "The principal subject of his inquiries was Deity ---The great First Cause, the Supreme Intelligence of the Universe. He concluded that nothing could pass from non-existence to existence. All things that exist are created by Supreme Intelligence who is Eternal and Immutable. A plurality of gods is impossible. With these sublime views: the unity and eternity and omnipotence of God, Xenophanes boldly attacked the popular errors of his day. He denounced the transference to the deity of the human form.

He believed in the One, which is God; not a personal God...but Deity pervading all space. He could not separate God from the World. There was no way to arrive at the truth, 'if error is spread over all things,' he said. It was not disdain of knowledge; it was the combat of contradictory opinions that oppressed him. He had attained recognition of the unit and perfections of God, and this conviction he would spread abroad, and tear down the superstitions which hid the face of truth.

I have great admiration for this philosopher; so sad, so earnest, so enthusiastic, wandering from city to city, indifferent to money, comfort, friends or fame that he might kindle the knowledge of God. This was a lofty aim for philosophy in that age."

<u>By John Lord, "Beacon Lights of History"</u>

**<u>Thomas Paine, "The Age of Reason:"</u>**
"Do we want to contemplate His power? We see it in the immensity of the Creation. Do we want to contemplate His wisdom? We see it in the unchangeable order by which the incomprehensible whole is governed. Do we want to contemplate His munificence? We see it in the

abundance with which He fills the Earth. Do we want to contemplate His mercy? We see it in His not withholding that abundance even from the ungrateful."

# Jesus, Paul and Believers:
## A Brief Comparison

**JESUS:** The Son of God whose sacrifice reconciled mankind to God.

**PAUL:** An apostle, teacher, and an example to follow.

**BELIEVERS:** They preach salvation on the merit of trusting in the Lord as their Savior.

**Jesus** "My Father works and I work."..."Jesus increased in wisdom and in stature, and in favor with God and man. ...The fame of him went out through all the region round about, and they were astonished at his doctrine for his word was with power. ...Jesus went up into the temple and taught, and the Jews marveled saying, 'How knows this man letters, having never learned?'...Jesus went about doing good."

**Paul** "In all things approve ourselves as the ministers of God: by pureness, by knowledge, by long-suffering, by kindness, by the Holy Spirit, by love unfeigned, by the word of truth, by the power of God, by the armor of righteousness..."

**Believers** (Evangelical Doctrine) "We receive the gift of eternal life through Jesus' sacrifice when we trust Him as our personal Savior. The Holy Spirit is given to us at that moment, and the believer becomes a saint. Our works are useless regarding salvation. God imputes righteousness to believers, and all sins are forgiven if we repent and confess them. We take our message of salvation to the unsaved."


## Advancing Christians

**Matthew 7-24, 25** "Whosoever hears these sayings of mine and does them, I will liken him to a wise man who built his house upon a rock. The rain descended, and the floods came, and the winds blew, and beat upon that house, and it fell not for it was founded upon a rock."

**Colossians 1-9, 10** "We pray for you and desire that you might be filled with the knowledge of His will in all wisdom and Spiritual understanding. That you might walk worthy of the Lord, unto all, pleasing. Be fruitful in good work and increase in the knowledge of God."

<u>Benjamin Franklin, "The Completed Autobiography:"</u>
"I do not desire to see faith diminished, nor would I endeavor to lessen it in any man. But I wish it were more productive of good works than I have generally seen it. I mean real good works. Acts of kindness, charity, mercy and public spirit; not holiday keeping, sermon reading or hearing; performing church ceremonies or making long prayers filled with flatteries and compliments, despised even by the wise men, and much less capable of pleasing the Deity...

If men rest in hearing and praying, as too many do, it is as if a tree should value itself on being watered and putting forth leaves; though it never produced any fruit."


<u>A Beginning</u>: "As many as received him, to them gave He the power to become sons of God."

The Endeavor: "As many as are guided by the Spirit of God, they are the sons of God...and if children, then heirs of God and joint-heirs with Christ."

The Outcome: "He loves them that follow after righteousness."

# Reverend John Wesley
(From two sermons)

### The Young Minister
"He that believes not is condemned already, and so long as he believes not, that condemnation cannot be removed, but 'the wrath of God abides on him.' As there is no other name given under Heaven than that of Jesus of Nazareth, there is no other merit whereby a condemned sinner can ever be saved from the guilt of sin. So that as long as we are without this faith, we are 'strangers to the covenant of promise.' We are 'aliens from the commonwealth of Israel, and without God in the world.'

Whatsoever good works he may do, it profits not; he is still a child of wrath, still under the curse, till he believes in Jesus. Faith therefore is the necessary condition of justification...The very moment God gives faith, for it is the gift of God 'to the ungodly that works not; that faith is counted to him for righteousness.' He has no righteousness at all, antecedent to this, not so much as negative righteousness or innocence. But 'faith is imputed to him for righteousness' the very moment he believes. As 'he made Christ to be sin for us,' that is, treated him as a sinner, punishing him for our sins; so He counts us righteous from the time we believe in him...treats us as though we were guiltless and righteous.

Surely the difficulty of assenting to the proposition that faith is the only condition of justification, must arise from not understanding it. Faith is the sole condition of justification. God sanctifies as well as justifies all them that believe in him...The righteousness of Christ is imputed to every believer."


### The Elder Statesman, Founder of Methodism
"Everyone has some measure of that light; some faint glimmering ray, which, sooner or later, more or less, enlightens every man that comes into the world. And everyone, unless he is one of the small number

whose conscience is seared with a hot iron, feels more or less uneasy when he acts contrary to the light of his own conscience. So that no man sins because he has not grace, but because he does not use the grace which he has.

Therefore inasmuch as God works in you, you are now able to work out your own salvation. Since he works in you of his own good pleasure, both to will and to do, it is possible for you to fulfill all righteousness.

God works in you; therefore you must work. You must be workers together with Him, otherwise He will cease working. The general rule on which His gracious dispensations invariably proceed is this: 'Unto him that hath, more shall be given.' Even St. Augustine makes that just remark, 'He that made us without ourselves will not save us without ourselves.' He will not save us unless we 'save ourselves from this untoward generation... unless we fight the good fight of faith, and lay hold on eternal life.'... 'Be you steadfast, immoveable; always abounding in the work of the Lord...and the God of peace, who brought again from the dead the great Shepherd of His sheep, make you perfect in every good work to do His will, working in you what is well-pleasing in His sight.'"

<u>Wesleyan Theology</u>, "Sermons"

# AN OPEN LETTER TO EVANGELICALS

Do consider the feasibility in examining doctrines passed down through the many years. We owe it to ourselves to search for a truth that is satisfying to the heart, rather than accepting without question the inheritance from nameless predecessors. When a person is ardently studying the New Testament, it becomes apparent that contradictions to teachings based on long ago formulated doctrines will appear, and they are not deeply hidden.

Many Scriptures of high significance have gone unnoticed, diluted or cast aside in favor of morale-boosters, and those that leave people secure, free from guilt, and unencumbered with motivation to improve facets of their lives.

<u>Underlined are Evangelical Doctrines. Descending are references in this book to compare with and seriously appraise alongside those old established norms.</u>

"<u>Everyone is saved if they trust in the Lord as their personal Savior.</u>"
    The Gospel of John
    "Salvation Indisputable," a list of scriptures.

"<u>Our works are useless; they cannot save us.</u>"
    Romans Chapter 3 and 4: a study.
    "The importance of good works," a list of scriptures.
    The Epistle of James.

"<u>God Imputes righteousness to believers.</u>"
    Romans Chapter 4: a study.
    "Our Righteousness," a list of scriptures.

"<u>He forgives all of our sins if we repent and confess them.</u>"
    Romans Chapter 6

Romans Chapter 7, victory over sin.
1 John

"<u>Believers are given the Holy Spirit, and became saints when they accept the Lord as their Savior.</u>"
    Acts 5-32
    Romans Chapter 8
    1 and 11 Corinthians

(The End Time) "<u>The Rapture is for people who have accepted Jesus as their personal Savior.</u>"
    <u>David</u>: Psalm 15
    <u>Jesus</u>: Matthew Chapter 24,
        John 5-28, 29
    <u>Paul:</u> 1 Thessalonians
    <u>Peter</u>: 2 Peter

# REFLECTIONS ON STUDYING THE NEW TESTAMENT

It is possible to understand, once and for all of time, what the Gospels and Epistles are teaching, and thereby not feel committed to spend a lifetime in 'Bible Study.' The benefit of having a reduced or an overview of each epistle, (as in this book of selections from the New Testament), is that key content will become increasingly meaningful, and more easily assimilated. (The original is presumed to be nearby for reference, clarification and additions.)

A concordance is a must for finding a specific Scripture when not recalling *where* a particular one is, by using a key word to locate it. At times, the simplest word will help identify a searched-for Scripture.

One example in considering the above: 'Mortify': Note how **Romans 8-13** and **Colossians 3-5, 6** extend the meaning with added detail:

> **'Romans' 8-13** "Through the Spirit, mortify the deeds of the body and you shall live."

> **Colossians 3-6** "Mortify your members upon the earth: covetous, uncleanness, malice, (and continuing with the phrase, "children of disobedience.")

'The point of agreement is that *obedience or following Spiritual guidance* shows there is assistance in overcoming temptations.

A good concordance will easily show what each of the Apostles had to say about the 'End Time' under the word 'End'. **Matthew 24** will be listed, and others will usually be in the margin of those referenced. KJV margin in **Matthew 24** lists **1 Thessalonians, chapters 4, 5** in which margin is **2 Peter 3-10** for his statements on the 'End Time.' That chapter-margin lists **Luke 12-40.**

Regardless of the above examples and other references available as well, many will still cling to, "Believe (or trust) in the Lord, and you will be saved."

<u>Another example of the feasibility in comparing Scripture to Scripture:</u> There are rich people who have acquired their wealth honestly. They may have read, "It is easier for a camel to go through the eye of a needle then for a rich man to enter the Kingdom of God." **Matthew 19-24.**

That image is moderated with a message on generosity. Paul's first Epistle to Timothy: "Charge them that are rich in this world, that they do good, that they are rich in good works, ready to distribute, willing to communicate; that they may lay hold on eternal life." **1 Timothy 6: 17-19.**

CHAPTER 2

# The Gospel of John: The Holy Spirit

Hearing and doing are imperative to believing.

**John 1-4** "In Him was life and the life was the light of men."

**John 1-9** "He was the true light that lights everyone who comes into the world. He came unto his own, and his own received him not. But as many as received him, to them gave he the power to become the sons of God."

>**Titus 2-11** "The grace of God that brings salvation has appeared unto all; teaching us that we should live soberly and righteously in this present world."

>Since "faith comes by hearing," many can relate an instance at some point of a passing thought that is intuitively sensed apart from oneself; perhaps in the form of a conveyed annoyance at one's own inconsiderate act; a quick insight of something that should be done, or an outright chastening. A strict mother of three said, "You should hear what He tells me."

>Robert Barclay, "An Apology for the True Christian Divinity."
"Let such know that the secret light which shines in the heart and reproves unrighteousness is the small beginning of the

revelation of God's Spirit, and as it is received and not resisted, works the salvation of all."

**John, Chapter 1** John (the Baptist) bare record, saying, "I saw the Spirit descending from Heaven like a dove, and it abode upon him. And I knew him not; but He that sent me to baptize with water, the same said unto me, 'Upon whom thou shalt see the Spirit descending, and remaining on him, the same is he which baptizes with the Holy Spirit.' And I saw, and bare record that this is the Son of God... And John the Baptist preached saying, 'Make straight the way of the Lord.'"

<u>The First Testimony Regarding the Holy Spirit, (Chapter 3).</u>
"There was a man of the Pharisees, named Nicodemus, a ruler of the Jews, who came to Jesus by night, and said unto him, 'Rabbi, we know that thou art a teacher come from God; for no man can do these miracles as thou does, except God be with him.'

Jesus answered, 'Verily, I say unto thee, except a man be born of water and the Spirit, he cannot enter into the Kingdom of God. That which is born of flesh is flesh; and that which is born of the Spirit is Spirit.'"

> Being born of water and the Spirit, implies a transformative work that prepares a person for "the Kingdom." No instant renovation is implied such as: "Trust in the Lord as your Savior, and you are born again." (A quote): "Religion should appeal to the mind as well as the heart." To address character improvements such as Peter described: "add to your faith, virtue, to virtue, kindness…; to follow Spiritual guidance as awareness heightens as well as the counsel of the written word including applicable Psalms and Proverbs; these are factors leading to the 'born again' or born anew status.

**1 Peter 1-22, 23 & 2-2** "Seeing you have purified your souls in obeying the Spirit...being born again by the word of God"...

**1 John 2-29**: "Everyone that does righteousness is born of God."

**JOHN 3-16, 18** "God so loved the world that He gave His only begotten Son, that whosoever believes in him should not perish, but have everlasting life... He that believes on him is not condemned, but he that believes not is condemned already because he has not believed in the name of the only begotten Son of God."

Many people find that believing is not instantaneous. Although they do want to believe; they cannot profess a faith that is not heartfelt; as someone said, "Believing cannot be coerced." Examples:

**Mark 9-24** ..."And straightway the father of the child cried out, and said with tears, 'Lord, I believe, I believe; help thou mine unbelief.'"

**Matthew 16-15, 16, 17** Jesus said unto them, "But whom say ye that I am?" Simon Peter answered, 'Thou art the Christ, the Son of the living God.' And Jesus answered, "Blessed art thou Simon, for flesh and blood has not revealed this unto you, but my Father who is in Heaven."

**John 3-19, 20, 21** ..."And this is the condemnation; that light is come into the world, and people loved darkness rather than light because their deeds were evil. For everyone who does evil hates the light, neither comes to the light lest his deeds should be reproved. But he that does truth, [*'does good'*, being opposite] comes to the light, that his deeds may be made manifest, that they are approved of God."

Proselytizers for 'winning souls' are remiss if they promote **John 3-16** for salvation, and ignore those immediate qualifying Scriptures.

<u>Other Scriptures on the subject of 'good' as imperative to salvation</u>:
**Proverbs 12-2** "A good person obtains favor of the Lord."
**Proverbs 28-18** "Whoso walks uprightly shall be saved."
**3 John 11** "Beloved, follow that which is good. He that does good is of God."

<u>Dhammapada, 5th Century B.C.</u>:
"Let no man think lightly of good, saying in his heart it will not come nigh unto me. Even by the falling of water-drops, a water-pot is filled. The wise man becomes full of good, even if he gathers it little by little."

<u>The Second Testimony Regarding the Holy Spirit. The Woman at the Well, (Chapter 4).</u>
"If thou knew the gift of God, and who it is that saith to thee, 'Give me to drink,' thou would have asked of him, and he would have given thee living water. ...Whosoever drinks of this water will thirst again, but whosoever drinks of the water that I shall give, will never thirst, but the water that I shall give will be a well of water springing up into everlasting life. True worshippers worship the Father in spirit and in truth for the Father seek such to worship Him....

....And many of the Samaritans believed on him for the saying of the woman who testified, 'He told me all that ever I did.'"

<u>R.A. Redford, "Vox Dei,"</u> *Doctrine of the Spirit*
"God is Spirit: and they that worship Him must worship Him in Spirit and in truth. It is not the Spirit without the

truth in which we worship God, nor is it the truth without the Spirit... Our Savior threw no disparagement upon sacred places or upon religious services by such words... He takes no delight in mere waves of feeling passing over the soul, nor will He accept the acknowledgment of a creed, or the intellectual assent to the truth in the abstract without Spiritual life. He is worshipped as a Spirit by a living communion; for a spirit can only worship Spirit by intelligent and loving interaction...Hence the Spirit is called the Spirit of Truth, and His work is to enlighten, to remove the darkness of ignorance and corruption; to reveal God to our spirits, and to lead us into fellowship with God."

<u>Scriptures, Chapter 5</u>
(The Gospel of John continues.)

<u>Hearing that which is spoken to each individual; a certainty to believing</u>.
**John 5-24** "He that hears my words, and believes on Him that sent me has everlasting life."
**John 5-25, 29** "The hour is coming when the dead will hear the voice of the Son of God, and all in the graves shall come forth... Those who have done good unto the resurrection of life..."

> **Matthew 12-35** "A good person out of the good treasure of the heart beings forth good things...
>
> <u>St. Augustine</u>: "Every being to the extent that it is a being at all, must have the attribute of goodness."

**John 5-39, 40** "Search the scriptures; for in them you think you have eternal life, and they do testify of me, but you will not come to me that you might have life."

"And lo, thou art unto them as a very lovely song; of one that has a pleasant voice, and can play well on an instrument: for they hear thy words, but they do them not." (Ezekiel 33-32)

**John 5-46** "Had you believed Moses, you would have believed me; for he wrote of me. But if you believe not his writings, how will you believe my words?"

<u>The Third Testimony Regarding the Holy Spirit: The Bread from Heaven, (Chapter 6).</u>
"Work not for the meat that perishes, but for that which endures unto everlasting life, which the Son of man shall give unto you…This is the work of God; that you believe on him whom he has sent." They said, 'what sign showest thou that we might see and believe thee? What dost thou work? Our fathers did eat manna in the desert…He gave them bread from Heaven to eat.'

Jesus said, "Moses gave you not that bread from Heaven; but my Father gives you the true bread from Heaven. For the bread of God is he which comes down from Heaven, and gives life unto the world…I am the bread of life; he that comes to me shall never hunger and he that believes on me shall never thirst. And this is the will of Him that sent me; that everyone who sees the Son and believes on him may have everlasting life, and I will raise him up at the last day."

The Jews then murmured at him because he said, 'I am the bread which came down from Heaven.' Jesus said, "Murmur not among yourselves…It is written in the prophets, 'and they shall be all taught of God'. Every man therefore that has heard, and has learned of the Father, comes unto me… Verily, I say unto you He that believes on me has everlasting life."

"I am the living bread of life which cometh down from Heaven, that a man may eat thereof and not die…He dwells in me and I in him." Many of the disciples said, "This is a hard saying; who can hear it?"

"It is the Spirit that quickens; the words that I speak unto you, are Spirit and are life."

(Paul on *dwelling in* and *quickens*):

**1 Corinthians 3-16** "Know you not that you are the temple of God, and the Spirit of God dwells in you?"

**Romans 8-13** "He shall also quicken you; therefore through the Spirit mortify the deeds of the body, and you shall live."

Robert Barclay:
"Philip Melancthon in his annotations upon John vi, 'Those who hear only an outward and bodily voice hear the creature, but God is a Spirit, and is neither discerned, nor known, nor heard, but by the Spirit, and therefore to hear the voice of God; to see God is to know and to hear the Spirit. By the Spirit alone God is known and perceived…Yea, all those who apply themselves effectually to Christianity, and are not satisfied until they have found its effectual work upon their hearts, redeeming them from sin, do feel that no knowledge effectually prevails to the producing of this, but that which proceeds from the influence of God's Spirit upon the heart…'"

**1 Peter 2-7** "Unto you who believe, he is honorable, but to the disobedient, a stone of stumbling…" (Considered interchangeable: 'believing' and 'obedience.')

Dietrich Bonhoeffer, "The Cost of Discipleship:"
"The step of obedience must be taken before faith can be possible…Unless he obeys, a man cannot believe. Are you worried because you find it so hard to believe? You are to perform the act of obedience on the spot. Then you will find yourself in the situation where faith becomes possible, and where faith exists in the true sense of the word."

## HIS WILL
### John Chapters 7 through 12,
### A selection:

**John 7-17** "If anyone will do His will, he shall know of the doctrine whether it be of God, or I speak of myself."

**7-37, 38, 39** "If anyone thirst, let him come unto me and drink. He that believes on me as the scripture has said, 'out of his belly will flow rivers of living water.' This he spoke of the Spirit which they that believe on him should receive; for the Holy Spirit was not now because Jesus was not yet glorified."

**John 8-12** "I am the Light of the world. He that follows me shall not walk in darkness, but shall have the light of life."

**8-31** "If you continue in my word, you are my disciples indeed, and you shall know the truth, and the truth shall make you free."

**8-34, 36** "Whosoever commits sin is the servant of sin…If the Son shall make you free, you shall be free indeed."

**8-47** "He that is of God hears God's words. You hear not because you are not of God."

**8-51** "If a person keep my sayings, he shall never see death."

**John 9-31** "If a person is a worshipper of God, and does his will, him he hears."

**John 10-27** "My sheep hear my voice and I know them, and they follow me, and I give unto them eternal life."

**John 12-2** "If anyone serve me, let them follow me."

<u>The Comforter</u>
<u>The Fourth Testimony of Jesus and the Holy Spirit.</u>
Addressing His Disciples:
"If you love me, keep my Commandments, and I will pray the Father, and He will give you another Comforter that he may abide with you forever; the Spirit of truth whom the world knows not but you know Him for He dwells with you, and shall be in you.

He that has my Commandments and keeps them, he it is that loves me, and he that loves me shall be loved of my Father, and I will love him and will manifest myself to him… If a man love me, he will keep my words, and my Father will love him, and we will come unto him, and make our abode with him…The word which you hear is not mine, but of the Father who sent me.

The Comforter, the Holy Spirit, whom the Father will send in my name shall teach you all things, and bring all things to your remembrance whatsoever I have said unto you. Hereafter I will not talk much with you; for the prince of this world comes and has nothing in me.

If you abide in me and my words abide in you, you shall ask what you will, and it shall be done unto you. Herein is my Father glorified that you bear much fruit; so shall you be my disciples. If you keep my Commandments, you shall abide in my love as I have kept my Father's Commandments, and abide in His love. This is my Commandment that you love one another, as I have loved you. You are my friends if you do whatsoever I command you. Henceforth I call you not servants; for the servant knows not what his Lord does, but I have called you friends for all things that I have heard of my Father, I have made know unto you… It is expedient that I go away; for if I go not away, the Comforter will not come unto you, but if I depart I will send him unto you. Howbeit when He, the Spirit of truth is come, He will guide you into all truth.

A little while, and you shall not see me, and again a little while, and you shall see me. I go to the Father."

CHAPTER 3

# The Acts of the Apostle

Honorable People

**Joseph** "A counselor; a good man, and just."

**Tabitha** "She was known for good works and alms deeds. She died and was restored to life by Peter who had kneeled and prayed.

> Peter said, 'Tabitha arise.' When she saw Peter, she sat up. He gave her his hand, and lifted her up...And then he called the saints and widows, and presented her alive."

**Cornelius** "A devout man and one that feared God, gave much alms to the people and prayed to God. He saw in a vision, an angel of God coming to him. He said unto him, Thy prayers and thine alms are come up for a memorial before God...."

**Barnabas** "A good man and full of the Holy Spirit and faith. He was sent to go to Antioch, who, when he came and had seen the grace of God was glad, and exhorted them all; that with purpose of heart they should cleave unto the Lord. And many were added unto the Lord."

**Lydia** "A seller of purple who worshipped God; heard us and whose heart the Lord opened that she attended unto the things that were spoken of by Paul."

**Ananias** "A devout man according to the Law, having a good report of all the Jews; instructed Paul that he was chosen, and that he should hear His voice and know His will."

**Apollos** "An eloquent man and mighty in the Scriptures: This man was instructed in the way of the Lord, and being fervent in the spirit, he spoke and taught diligently the things of the Lord. Aquila and Priscilla heard him speak boldly in the synagogue, and they took him aside and expounded to him the way of God more perfectly. He mightily convinced the Jews, opening Scriptures to them."

**Timothy** "A certain disciple who was well-reported of by the brethren. Him would Paul have to go forth with him. And they went through the cities delivering to them the decree to keep those things ordained of the Apostles and the elders."

**Stephen** "A man full of faith and the Holy Spirit and power; did great wonders and miracles among the people. There arose certain of the synagogue who disputed with Stephen. And they were not able to resist the wisdom and the Spirit by which he spoke. And all that sat in the council looking steadfastly on him, saw his face as if it had been the face of an angel."

## The Acts of the Apostles
One Scripture clarifies another.

### On Salvation and the 'End Time:'
**Acts 2-20, 21 (Peter)** "The sun shall be turned into darkness; the moon into blood before that great and notable day of the Lord come, and it shall come to pass that whosoever shall call on the name of the Lord will be saved.

**11 Peter 3-11, 14** "Seeing all these things will be dissolved, what manner of persons should you be in all holy conversation and godliness? Be diligent to be found of Him… blameless."

**Matthew 7-31** "Not everyone who says unto me 'Lord, Lord' shall enter the Kingdom of Heaven, but they that do the will of my Father who is in Heaven."

### The Holy Spirit is given:
**Acts 2-38 Peter** "Repent and be baptized for the remission of sins, and you will receive the gift of the Holy Spirit."
**Acts 5-32 Peter** "God has given the Holy Spirit to them that obey Him."
**Acts 15-8 Peter** "God who knows the hearts, gave them the Holy Spirit, even as unto us."

### On Sin:
**Acts 4-18, 26 PETER** "Repent and be converted that your sins may be blotted out… God sent His Son to bless you in turning away every one of you from his iniquities."

**1 Corinthians 15-57:** "…Thanks be to God who gives us the victory through our Lord."

**2 Timothy 2-19** "Let everyone who names the name of Christ depart from iniquity."

<u>Peter's Vision:</u>

**Acts 10** "Peter saw a 'vision' along with a voice which said: 'What God has cleansed, call not thou common or unclean.' (The Gentiles would no longer be denied acceptance with God.)

**Acts 10-28 (Peter)** "You know how that it is an unlawful thing for a man that is a Jew to keep company or to come unto one of another nation, but God has showed me that I should not call any man common or unclean."

**Acts 10-34 (Peter)** "Of a truth, I perceive that God is no respecter of persons: but in every nation, he that fears Him and works righteousness is acceptable to Him."

**Acts 10-43 (Peter)** "To Him give all the Prophets witness, that through His name whosoever believes in Him shall receive remission of sins." (Indicating that 'remission of sins' would not be limited to the Jews: (with 10-34).

**Acts 10-45** "Those of the circumcision who believed were astonished, as many as came with Peter, because that on the Gentiles also was poured out the gift of the Holy Spirit."

**Acts 11-1** "And the Apostles and brethren that were in Judea heard that the Gentiles had also received the word of God."

**Acts 13-38, 39 (Paul)** "By Him, all that believe are justified from all things, from which you could not be justified by the Law of Moses." (Again, the faith/Law comparison. Acts 10-34 continues to apply.)

**Acts 14-22** ..."Exhorting them to continue in the faith, and that we must through much tribulation enter into the Kingdom of God."

**Acts 15-7, 8** "**Peter** rose up and said that the Gentiles should hear the word of the gospel and believe. And God, who knows the hearts, gave them the Holy Spirit even as unto us; and put no difference between us and them, purifying their hearts by faith."

**1 Peter 1-22** "You have purified your souls in obeying ... the Spirit."

<u>The Essence:</u>

1. Access to God would no longer be denied to the Gentiles.
2. The Jews would find justification through faith as opposed to relying on their Law, "the Law of Moses," to gain approval.
3. The above should not be extended into the presumption that all believers are acceptable to God.

**Acts 16 (Paul)** (*The <u>Philippian</u>* jailor's conversion): "Sirs, what must I do to be saved? And they said, 'Believe on the Lord Jesus, and thou shalt be saved, and thy house.' And they spoke unto them the word of the Lord, and to all that were in his house."

<u>Paul's *Epistle* to the Philippians</u>: "Work out your own salvation; for it is God who works in you both to will and to do those things that are acceptable to Him."

**Acts 17 (Paul)** "They came to <u>*Thessalonica,*</u> and Paul went with them to the synagogue of the Jews, and for three Sabbath days reasoned with them out of the scriptures..."That this Jesus whom I preach unto you is Christ."

In Paul's *first Epistle to the* <u>Thessalonians</u>: "We exhorted every one of you as a father to his children that you would walk worthy of God...Hold fast that which is good, and your whole spirit and soul and body be preserved blameless unto the coming of the Lord."

**Acts 19-8, 10** "And he went into the synagogue, and spoke boldly for the space of three months, disputing and persuading the things concerning the Kingdom of God...And this continued by the space of two years...so that all they which dwelt in Asia heard the word of the Lord Jesus; both Jews and Greeks."

> When Paul 'persuaded' in the synagogue on requirements for *Salvation*, it may be presumed that he included those same principles in his Epistles.
> See "Salvation Indisputable."

**Acts 24, Paul** said, "Herein do I exercise myself to have always a conscience void of offence toward God and man." He reasoned of righteousness, temperance and the judgment to come.

# Salvation Indisputable

**Romans 2** "To those who in well-doing seek immortality, eternal life…"
**1 Corinthians 6** "Know you not that the unrighteous shall not inherit the Kingdom of God?"
**Galatians 6** "Be not deceived… for whatsoever a person sows; that shall he also reap."
**Ephesians 6-17** "…And take the helmet of salvation, and the sword of the Spirit which is the word of God.
**Philippians 2** "Work out your own salvation, for it is God who works in you both to will and to do of his pleasure."
**Colossians 3** "He that does wrong shall receive for the wrong which he has done, and there is no respect of persons with God."
**11 Thessalonians 2** "They received not the love of the truth that they might be saved… But had pleasure in unrighteousness."
**1 Timothy 2** "Lead a peaceable life in all uprightness and honesty; for this is good and acceptable to God who would have everyone saved and come to the knowledge of the truth."
**Titus 2** "The grace of God that brings salvation has appeared to all men teaching us that denying ungodliness, we should live soberly and righteously in this present world."

CHAPTER 4

# Paul's Epistle to the Romans, Chapters 1 and 2

"Believe by the things that are made."
His judgment is against unrighteousness.

**Romans 1** "We have received grace and apostleship for obedience to the faith among all nations. I am ready to preach the gospel to you that are at Rome also. The Gospel is the power of God unto salvation to everyone that believes; to the Jew first and also to the Greek. For therein is the righteousness of God revealed as it is written, "The just shall live by faith."

"…to everyone that believes" refers to the teaching of the Gospel.

> **1 Corinthians**…"I declared unto you the Gospel wherein you stand if you keep in memory what I preached; unless you believed in vain."

**Romans 1: 8-20** …."For the wrath of God is against all ungodliness and unrighteousness of men who hold the truth in unrighteousness because that which may be known of God is manifest in them, for God hath shown it unto them. For the invisible things of Him from the Creation of the world are clearly seen being understood by the things that are made: His eternal power and Godhead; so they are without excuse."

Plato: "The Earth, the Sun and Stars, and the Universe itself, and the charming variety of the seasons, demonstrate the existence of a Divinity."

De Legibus, Lib. X1, 4th C. B.C.

Galileo: "When I consider how many and how great mysteries men have understood, discovered and contrived, I very plainly know and understand that the mind of man to be one of the works of God, yea, one of the most excellent."

Dialogue on the Great World Systems,

Pascal: "Let man then contemplate the whole of Nature in her full and lofty Majesty. Let him turn his gaze away from the lowly objects around him. Let him behold the dazzling light set like an eternal lamp to light up the Universe. Nature is an infinite sphere whose center is everywhere and circumference nowhere. In short it is the greatest perceptible mark of God's omnipotence."

Pensees'

S.T. Coleridge: "The wonderful works of God in the sensible World are a perpetual discourse reminding me of His existence, and shadowing out to me His perfections."

Aids to Reflection.

**Romans 1: 21-32** ... "When they knew God, they glorified Him not as God, neither were they thankful, but became vain in their imaginations, and their foolish heart was darkened. Professing themselves to be wise, they became fools...And changed the glory of the incorruptible God into an image made like to corruptible man, and four-footed beasts...Wherefore God also gave them up to uncleanness through the lusts of their own hearts, to dishonor their own bodies between themselves...men with men working that which is unseemly....

Being filled with all unrighteousness, fornication, wickedness, covetousness, maliciousness, full of envy, murder, deceit, malignity, backbiters, haters of God,… inventors of evil things…who know the judgment of God, that they which commit such things are worthy of death, not only do the same, but have pleasure in them that do them."

**Romans 2: 4-6** "Despise thou the riches of His goodness and forbearance and longsuffering; not knowing that the goodness of God leads thee to repentance? But after thy hard and impenitent heart, treasure up unto thyself wrath against the day of wrath, and revelation of the righteous judgment of God, who will render to every man according to his deeds:

**Romans 2:7-11** …To them who by patient continuance in well-doing, seek for glory and honor and immortality: eternal life. But unto them that are contentious, and do not obey the truth, but obey unrighteousness: indignation and wrath. Tribulation and anguish upon every soul of man that does evil, of the Jew first and also of the Gentile. But glory, honor and peace to everyone who works good. For there is no respect of persons with God.

**Romans 2-14,15** When the Gentiles who have not the Law, do by nature the things contained in the Law, these having not the Law, are a law unto themselves: who show the work of the Law written in their hearts, their conscience also bearing witness, and their thoughts meanwhile accusing or excusing one another."

W. R. Forester, "Christian Vocation:"
"If we believe that God speaks to real persons in guidance and learning, we must believe that the Christian conscience is the voice of God, determining my duty here and now."

**Romans 2:17-29** "Behold, thou art called a Jew and rest in the Law, and make thy boast of God, and know His will, and approve things that are more excellent being instructed out of the Law, and are confident that thou art a guide of the blind, a light of them who are in darkness…

Thou therefore which teach another, teach not thyself? Thou that preach a man should not steal, dost thou steal? ...Should not commit adultery, dost thou? ...Thou that make thy boast of the Law, through breaking the Law, dishonor thou God? ...For he is not a Jew, who is one outwardly, but he is a Jew who is one inwardly; in the spirit and not in the letter of the Law."

# God Speaks To Job

From: <u>The Book of Job:</u>

..."Then the Lord answered Job out of the whirlwind and said, 'Who is this that darkens counsel by words without knowledge? Gird up now thy loins like a man; for I will demand of thee, and answer thou me. Where were thou when I laid the foundations of the Earth? Declare, if thou hast understanding. Who has laid the measures thereof, if thou know? Or who hath stretched the line upon it? Whereupon are the foundations thereof fastened? Or who laid the corner stone thereof; or who shut up the sea with doors, when it brake forth?

Hast thou commanded the morning since thy day, and caused the dayspring to know his place? Has thou perceived the breadth of the Earth? Declare if thou know it all. Who hath divided a watercourse for the overflowing of waters, or a way for the lightning of thunder; to cause it to rain on the earth where no man is-- on the wilderness wherein there is no man.

Know thou the ordinances of Heaven? Canst thou set the dominion thereof in the Earth? Canst thou lift up thy voice to the clouds that abundance of waters may cover thee? Who hath put wisdom in the inward parts? Or who hath given understanding to the heart?

Gave thou the goodly wings unto the peacocks? Or wings and feathers unto the ostrich?

Hast thou given the horse strength? Hast thou clothed his neck with thunder? He paws in the valley and rejoices in his strength. He goes on to meet the armored men. He mocks at fear, and is not affrighted.

Doth the hawk fly by thy wisdom, and stretch her wings toward the south? Doth the eagle mount up at thy command,

and make her nest on high? She dwells and abides on the rock, and upon the crag of the rock...and her eyes behold afar off.

Shall he that contends with the Almighty instruct him? He that reproves God, let him answer it."

> Then Job answered the Lord, and said, "Behold, I am vile; what shall I answer thee? I will lay mine hand upon my mouth. Once have I spoken, but I will not answer; yea, twice; but I will proceed no further."

"Then answered the Lord unto Job out of the whirlwind, and said, 'Gird up thy loins now like a man: I will demand of thee, and declare thou unto me. Wilt thou also disannul my judgment? Wilt thou condemn me, that thou may be righteous? Hast thou an arm like God? Or canst thou thunder with a voice like Him? Deck thyself now with majesty and excellency, and array thyself with glory and beauty. Cast abroad the rage of thy wrath: and behold every one that is proud, and abase him, and tread down the wicked in their place...Then will I also confess unto thee that thine own right hand can save thee.'"

# Paul's Epistle to the Romans, Chapters 3 and 4
"Not of works" refers to the Jewish Law.

The references to the Israelites' <u>*works of the* law</u> are noted predominately in Paul's Epistles to the <u>Romans and Galatians</u>. In those two letters Paul counseled his brethren most ardently to a life of faith; that the Law was imperative during the era before Christ when a 'schoolmaster' was needed for guidance toward righteousness, "until we might be justified by faith."

<u>Works of the Law only are addressed. (Good works harbor no negatives.)</u>

In the following portion of his letter, Paul wrote to his brethren regarding the superiority of faith over the Israelites' works of their Law. In referring to the Law, he states, "not of works," while explaining that justification now comes by faith. In the following scriptures from Chapters three and four, the subject of works pertains *only* to the Law and does not of a sudden, digress to the subject of works in general or to good works.

The digression does *appear* to occur, and the impact has been a negativity toward *good works* which is tragic because the end result in the minds of many who have believed it and preach or practice the same, conclude that, "our works are useless." Since good works are held in a dim light by many believers, Spiritual growth stalls because many fine attributes, hard to come by perhaps, are truly 'good works.'

<u>Two Scriptures from among many showing the importance of good works:</u>

**Titus 3-8** "These things I will that thou affirm constantly; that they who believe in God might be careful to maintain good works. These things are good and profitable unto man."
**James 2-24** "A man is justified by works and not by faith only."

## The analysis in order to intercept the disparagment of *good works*:

That the subject of 'works' pertains to the law is obvious with **3-20** through **3-31**; however with **4-2 through 4-6**, doubt may be kindled as to the type of works because the word *law* is omitted. Adding to that doubt is the fact that the chapter changes from three to four.

As one studies **chapter 4**, it becomes evident that the subject, works of the Law does in fact continue, as is proven by the final brief review of **4-13, 14 and 16** using the words: 'for' and 'therefore' with return of the word 'Law'. To conclude: the negative connotation on *works*, from beginning to end, pertains to the Israelites' Law whether or not with each scripture, 'of the law' is included. ('Good works' and 'fruit bearing' never harbor a negative connotation anywhere in the New Testament.)

## A line by line study confirming that *works* therein pertains only to the Israelites' Law.

**Romans 3-20** "By the works of the Law no one shall be justified in His sight.
**3-21, 22, 26** But now the righteousness of God without the Law is manifest; the righteousness of God by faith in Jesus.
**3-27** Where is boasting then? It is excluded. By what Law, of works? No, by the law of faith.
**3-28** Therefore we conclude that a person is justified by faith without the works of the Law.
**3-31** Do we make void the law through faith? God forbid, yea, we establish the Law."

*Note*: See paragraph at the end titled, "How faith, establishes the Law."

**Romans 4-2, 4-3**..."For if Abraham were justified by works, he has reason to glory...For what saith the Scripture: Abraham believed God and it was counted unto him for righteousness.

> **(James 2: 21, 22, 24)** "Was not Abraham our Father justified by works when he had offered up Isaac his son upon the altar? You see then how faith wrought with his works, and by works was faith made perfect? You see then how that by works a man is justified, and not by faith only."

**4-4** "Now to him that works is the reward not reckoned of grace, but of debt.
**4-5** But to him that works not, but believes on him...his faith is counted for righteousness.
**4-6** Even as David also described the blessedness of the man unto whom God imputed righteousness without works."

**Romans 4-13, 14** ..."For the promise, that he should be heir of the world was not to Abraham...through their Law, but through the righteousness of faith.
**4-16**. Therefore, it is of faith that the promise might be to all; not to that only who are of the Law, but to those also who are of faith." (The above scriptures resolve the fact that the subject 'of the law' continues throughout; that the negative connotation toward 'works,' in Chapters 3 and 4 refers to the Israelite's "works of the law".)

(Completing the subject in the Romans' Epistle):

> **Romans 11-5 and 6** "There is a remnant according to the election of grace. If by grace, then is it no more of works, (referring to their Law) otherwise grace is no more grace." (Although the chapter changed from 10 to 11, this scripture continues

Paul's writing on the *works of the Law* compared to *faith*; that being the focal point of Chapters 9 and 10, in appealing to his brethren.

    Clarifying the same in Paul's other Epistles:
**Galatians 2-16** "A man is not justified by the works of the Law. We have believed in Jesus that we might be justified by faith and not by the works of the Law."
    (This is a welcome clarification).

**Ephesians 2-8, 9, 10** (Addressing both types of work): "By grace are you saved through faith, and that not of yourself, it is the gift of God; not of works, lest anyone should boast, for we are his workmanship created in Christ Jesus unto good works which God has before ordained that we should walk in them."

**2 Timothy 1-9** "He has saved us, and called us, not according to our works, but according to his own purpose and grace."

    Again, the subject of *works*, refers to their Law. It *is* significant that Paul wrote also regarding the Law in the first chapter of his first Epistle to Timothy.

    Further evidence that (negative) works applies to their Law; note how *good works* are upheld in two other Scriptures of the same Epistle:

    **2 Timothy 2-21** ..."If a person purge himself from these, he shall be a vessel unto honor, sanctified and fit for the master's use, and prepared for every good work."

**2 Timothy 3-16** "All scripture is given by inspiration of God, and is profitable for doctrine, for reproof, for correction, for instruction in righteousness; that the man of God be thoroughly furnished unto all good works."

The following Scriptures refer only to the Israelites' Law:

1. Works of the Law: **Romans 3-20** "By the works of the Law, no one is justified in his sight."
2. Law for Righteousness: **Romans 10-4** "Christ is the end of the law for righteousness"...
3. Righteousness of the Law: **Philippians 3-9** "To be found of him, not having my own righteousness which is of the Law, but the righteousness of God by faith."
4. Works *of* Righteousness: **Titus 3-5** "Not by works of righteousness we have done, but according to his mercy, he saved us; by the washing of regeneration and renewal of the Holy Spirit."

*Important key point for '4'*: Not to be confused with *works righteousness*:

**Acts 10-34, 35** "God is no respecter of persons, but in every nation he that works righteousness is acceptable to Him.

(Returning to): Romans 3-31: "...Faith establishes the Law":

"What must I do to inherit life?" "What does the Law say?" "To love the Lord... to love thy neighbor as thyself." "Thou hast answered right. This do and thou shalt live."
                                        **Luke 10: 25-28**

**Romans** 8-4 "The righteousness of the Law is fulfilled in us who *walk*... after the Spirit."

Faith thereby establishes the righteousness of the Law if that faith is active; either by a Spiritual walk, or **Romans 2-14**: ..."If the Gentiles do by nature those (upright and good) things contained in the law."

Robert Barclay:

"Faith in its proper signification means making one just; not merely reputing one such."

# The Importance of Good Works

**James' Epistle:**
**2-14** "What does it profit, though a person says he has faith and has not works? Can faith save him?
**2-17** Faith, if it has not works is dead, being alone.
**2-18** A person may say, 'thou has faith, and I have works.' Show me thy faith without thy works, and I will show thee my faith by my works.
**2-19, 20** Thou believes there is one God; thou doeth well; but wilt thou know, O vain man that faith without works is dead?
**2-21, 22**…Was not Abraham our father justified by works when he offered Isaac, his son on the altar? See then how faith wrought with his works, and by works was faith made perfect?
**2-24**…You see then how by works a person is justified, and not by faith only."

**Peter's Epistle:**
**1 Peter 1-17** …"The Father, who without respect of persons, judges according to everyone's work…
**1 Peter 2-12** Have your conversation honest among the Gentiles; that if they speak against you as evildoers, they may by your good works, glorify God."

**Paul's Epistles**:
**2 Corinthians 9-6, 8** "He who sows sparingly shall reap also sparingly, and he who sows bountifully shall reap also bountifully. May you abound in every good work."
**Galatians 6-10** "As we have therefore opportunity let us do good unto all."
**Ephesians 2-10** "We are his workmanship created unto good works. God has before ordained that we should walk in them."

**Philippians 4-16, 17** "You sent once and again unto my necessity, not because I desire a gift, but I desire fruit that may abound to your account."

**Colossians 1-10** ..."That you might walk worthy of the Lord, unto all pleasing; being fruitful in every good work."

**2 Thessalonians 2-16, 17** "Now our Lord comfort your hearts, and establish you in every good word and work."

**1 Timothy 5-9, 10** "A widow...well reported for good works if she has lodged strangers, if she has cared for the afflicted; if she has diligently followed every good work."

**2 Timothy 2-21** "He shall be a vessel unto honor, sanctified, and fit for the master's use, and prepared unto every good work."

**Hebrews 10-24** "Let us consider one another to provoke unto love and good works."

**Hebrews 13-20, 21** "Now, the God of peace...make you perfect in every good work to do His will, working in you that which is pleasing in His sight."

# Paul's Epistle to the Romans, Chapter 4
Abraham's obedience imputed him, "a righteous man."

The emphasis on Romans' *Chapters 3 and 4*, was to prove that all scriptures containing the word, *works* refer to the Israelite's Law, rather than *good works*.

The following dwells on *Chapter 4* only. The subject: "The imputation of righteousness."

Does God impute righteousness to believers; to those who say they are saved because they trust in the Lord? This is a commonly held belief.

There are those who maintain that people are incapable of becoming righteous by self-effort; therefore they must depend on God to impute righteousness to them. They draw on the Old Testament prophet Isaiah's writing to confirm their supposition:

**Isaiah 64-5, 6** "Behold, thou art wroth, for we have sinned. We are all as unclean, and all our righteousnesses are as filthy rags, and we all do fade as a leaf, and our iniquities like the wind, have taken us away."

Opposing Scriptures:

**Deuteronomy 6-25** "It shall be our righteousness if we do those things which He commands of us."
**Acts 10-34** "In every nation he that fears Him, and works righteousness is accepted with Him."

Faith, Paul tries to convince them, should be the principle for which they strive; wherein they will be guided toward a genuine, and productive righteousness; one that emulates God's own righteousness.

It is important to note the inter-changeable use of the words: *imputed, counted and accounted.* In Galatians 3-6: "Abraham believed God, and it was accounted to him for righteousness." In studying the upcoming scriptures in chapter four, one realizes that God did not impute righteousness to Abraham, but that he earned, on the merit of his obedience, accounted or imputed *a righteous man.*

**Romans 4-2, 3** "If Abraham were justified by works (of the law; the subject at hand), he has reason to glory. He believed God, and it was counted unto him for righteousness."
**Romans 4-11, 12** "Abraham was reckoned the father of all those that believe; that righteousness might be imputed to others also who walk in the steps of that faith of Abraham.
**Romans 4-19, 20, 21, 22** ..."And being not weak in faith, he considered not his own body when he was about a hundred years old, nor Sarah's age. He staggered not at the promise of God through unbelief, but was strong in faith being fully persuaded that what He had promised, He was able also to perform, and therefore it, was imputed to him for righteousness.
**Romans 4-23** "Now it was not written for his sake alone, that it was imputed to him; but for us also it shall be imputed, if we believe on him that raised up Jesus our Lord from the dead."

Abraham's belief was considerably different from that practiced and preached by many who call themselves believers in recent ages. Abraham followed God's will, and thereby gained His acceptance. He left his homeland, trusting; not knowing where he was going.

The qualifier for our being 'imputed or accounted righteous,' Paul stated: ..."*to others also who walk in the steps of that faith of Abraham.*"

### The obedience of Abraham to the will of God:

**Genesis 26-4, 5** "I will make thy seed to multiply as the stars of Heaven, and I will give unto thy seed all these countries, and in thy seed shall all the nations of the earth be blessed, because that Abraham obeyed my voice, and kept my charge; my Commandments."

**Hebrews 11-8** "By faith, Abraham when he was called to go out into a place which he should after receive for an inheritance, obeyed, and he went out not knowing whither he went."

**Hebrews 11-17** "By faith, Abraham when he was tried, offered up Isaac... his only begotten son."

## ABRAHAM

By John Lord:

"With the growth of cities and the power of kings, idolatry increased and knowledge of the true God declined. From such influences it was necessary that Abram should be removed if he was to found a nation with a monotheistic belief.

So in obedience to a call from God, he left the city of his birthplace, and went toward the land of Canaan. The Bible recognizes in Abram moral rather than intellectual greatness. He was distinguished for his faith, and a faith so exalted and pure that it was accounted to him for righteousness. His faith in God was so profound that it was followed by unhesitating obedience to His commands. He gave a religion to the world; at least he established its fundamental principle: the worship of the only true God.

If I were to analyze the faith of Abraham, I should say that it is a perfect trust in God allied with obedience to his commands. Religious faith is supreme trust in an unseen God, and supreme obedience to His commands."

## FAITH PROGRESSING TO A "WALK IN THE SPIRIT."

**Romans 5-5** "The love of God is shed abroad in our hearts by the Holy Spirit which is given unto us."
**Romans 7-6** "Now we are delivered from the Law; that we should serve in newness of spirit."
**Romans 8-4** ..."That the righteousness of the Law (those upright principles), might be fulfilled in us who walk after the Spirit."
**Romans 8-13** "If you through the Spirit mortify the deeds of the body, you shall live."
**1 Corinthians 6-9, 11** "Know you not that the unrighteous shall not inherit the Kingdom of God? And such were some of you, but you are washed, but you are sanctified, you are justified in the name of the Lord; and by the Spirit of God."
**Galatians 5-16** "If you walk in the Spirit, you will not fulfill the desires of the flesh."
**Ephesians 5-9** "The fruit of the Spirit is in all goodness and righteousness and truth."

### Our Righteousness

"He bore our sins in his own body... that we should live unto righteousness." (1 Peter 2-24)
"Righteousness leads to Holiness and the end: Everlasting life." (Romans 6)
"Awake to righteousness, and sin not." (1 Corinthians 15-34)
"The unrighteous shall not inherit the Kingdom of God." (1 Corinthians 6-9)
"The way of righteousness is life." (Proverbs 12-28)
"I am persuaded that you are full of Goodness." (Romans 15-14)
"Blessed are they that do righteousness at all times." (Psalm 106-3}

"Flee youthful lusts. Call on the Lord with a pure heart." (2 Timothy 2-22}
"Live soberly, righteously and godly in this present world." (Titus 2-12)
"Noah obeyed God, and became an heir of righteousness." (Hebrews 11-7}
"The effectual fervent prayer of the righteous avails much." (James 5-16)
"He that does righteousness is born of God." (1 John 2-29)
"He loves him that follows after righteousness." (Proverbs 15-9)
"The heart of the righteous studies to answer." (Proverbs 15-28)
"He hears the prayer of the righteous." (1 Peter 3-12)
"The lips of the righteous feed many." (Proverbs 10-21)
"They that turn many to righteousness shall shine as the stars forever and ever." (Daniel 12-3) "The Lord rewarded me according to my righteousness"... (Psalm 18-20)
"The fruit of the righteous is a tree of life." (Proverbs 11-30)
"The righteous person regards the life of his animal." (<u>Proverbs 12-10)</u>

They watch over the needs of the pet. They do not let a young child stress it. They add variety to the diet by sharing good quality food with them.

"Fathers provoke not your children to anger, lest they become discouraged." (<u>Colossians 3-21</u>)

A loving father now, will have a friend or two who cares about him in his later years. Recollections of good times, gentleness, conversation fine-tuned by reading, and doing things of interest with them will become endearing memories.

"She rises while it is still night, [in the winter] and gives food to her family. She looks well to the ways of her household." (Proverbs 31 15, 27)

> She would never send her children to school without breakfast. She listens when they want to share an important-to-them experience. With a love for reading and good music, she has learned to speak of the good, of history, of nature; of the ordinary, too. "…and her children will arise and call her blessed." (Proverbs 31-28).

# Paul's Epistle to the Romans, Chapter 5
"He bore our sins; therefore we should live unto righteousness."

**Romans 5a** "The love of God is shed in our hearts by the Holy Spirit which is given to us."

"God commended His love toward us, in that while we were yet sinners, Christ died for us. Much more then, being now justified by his blood, we shall be saved from wrath through him. For if when we were enemies, we were reconciled to God by the death of His Son, much more, being reconciled, we shall be saved by his life."

> **1 Peter 2-24, and 4-2** "He bore our sins in his own body on the tree that we should live unto righteousness."

> **Colossians 1: 21-23** "You that were sometime alienated and enemies… yet now has he reconciled in the body of his flesh through death, to present you holy and blameless… in his sight, if you continue in the faith and are not moved from the gospel which you have heard."

**Romans 5b.** "By one man, sin entered into the world and death reigned from Adam to Moses. As by the offence of one, judgment came upon all to condemnation; even so by the righteousness of one, the gift came upon all unto justification of life. For as by one man's disobedience, many were made sinners, so by the obedience of one, many shall be made righteous."

(The conclusion):

1. "We were reconciled to God by the death of His Son."
2. "He was raised again for our justification."
3. "Many shall be made righteous… by the Holy Spirit which is given to us."

**Titus 2:11-14** "The grace of God appearing unto all, teaches us that we should live righteously and godly in this present world. He gave Himself for us that He might redeem us from iniquity, and purify for himself a special people zealous of good works."

Karl Adam, "The Spirit of Catholicism."
"Justification is not a mere covering over of sin...It is the communication of a true inward righteousness; of a new love which remakes the whole man. It is sanctification."

William Law, "Christian Perfection."
"It would be strange to suppose that mankind were redeemed by the sufferings of their Savior, to live in ease and softness themselves."

# Paul's Epistle to the Romans, Chapter 6
"Yield to God as instruments of righteousness."

**6-1 through 6-11** "What shall we say then? Shall we continue in sin that grace may abound? God forbid!"

As Christ died for our sins, we should reckon ourselves to be dead also unto sin. Likewise, as he was raised from the dead and is alive unto God, we should reckon ourselves alive also to walk in newness of life."

> Uppermost in mind should remain this new revelation that, "the Holy Spirit is given," and, "many shall be made righteous."
>
> Many people take Chapter 5 as the end of the matter on salvation, now having a Savior who paid for our sins and reconciled us to God.
>
> With Chapter 6 and continuing, Christians are in the limelight for taking further instructions to heart as grateful learners rather than leaners; determining what changes are needed to become acceptable, if not beloved. Even acts of consideration are tokens of fineness of character progressing. The more we are inclined for purity in life, the more assistance is likely since, "He discerns the thoughts and intents of the heart."
>
> The yearning to do better and 'walk worthy' is in essence, a prayer for help. "Whatsoever we ask, we receive of Him, if we keep His Commandments and do those things that are pleasing in His sight."

**6-12 through 6-22** "Therefore, let not sin reign within you in obeying it. Neither yield to unrighteousness, but yield unto God as instruments of righteousness. Know you not that to whom you yield as servants to obey, his servants you are to whom you obey; whether of sin unto death, or of obedience leading to righteousness?

You were the servants of sin, but you have obeyed that form of doctrine which was delivered to you. Being made free from sin then, you began serving righteousness."

**Acts 3-26** "He sent Jesus to bless you, in turning away every one of you from his iniquities."

"As you have yielded to uncleanness and to iniquity; so now yield as servants of righteousness unto holiness.

When you obeyed sin, you were free from righteousness. What fruit had you then in those things you are now ashamed? For the end of those things is death.

But now being made free from sin, and become servants to God, you have your fruit unto holiness and the end, everlasting life."

The *twice*-stated in chapter 6: "Being made free from sin, you became servants of righteousness," and once in chapter 5, "many shall be made righteous," indicate an ongoing work.

**6-23** "The wages of sin is death, but the gift of God is eternal life through Jesus, our Lord."

His gifts to humanity include assistance in advancing toward righteousness.
**6-23** should not be quoted for one-line 'conversion' messages. By remaining in the context of this chapter: by yielding to the Holy Spirit; ("through Jesus" risen), righteousness advances with the ultimate reward of eternal life.

"On Romans Chapter Six," by Martin Luther:
"Throughout our lives we shall be kept fully employed with our own selves; taming our body, killing its passions, controlling its

members till they obey, not the passions, but the spirit...It is one thing to be provoked of the flesh, and yet not willing to yield to the lusts thereof. To walk after the leading of the Spirit, and resist the flesh, is optimum."

# PAUL'S EPISTLE TO THE ROMANS, CHAPTER 7
How to overcome sin, perplexed him.

**Romans 7-6** "Now we are delivered from the Law... that we should serve in newness of spirit, and not in oldness of the letter."

Whether Paul was writing from experience, or in a parable, attempts to defeat the problem of sin were futile.

**7-12 to 7-24** "The Commandment is holy, just and good. We know that the Law is spiritual, but I am carnal; sold under sin. For what I would do, I do not, but what I hate; that do I... Now then, it is no more I that do it, but sin that dwells in me...To will is present; but how to perform that which is good, I find not...Oh wretched man that I am! Who shall deliver me from the body of this death?
**7-25** I thank God through Jesus Christ, our Lord. So then with the mind, I serve the 'law' of God, but with the flesh, the 'law' of sin."

**Philippians 2-5, 8** "Let this mind be in you which was also in Christ Jesus: He humbled himself and became obedient..."

**Romans 8-13** "If you, through the Spirit, mortify the deeds of the body, you shall live."

William Kingsland, "Our Infinite Life":
"Intellect, we shall put in its proper place as complementary to the subjective life of the Spirit."

Rabbi Nahman of Bratslav: "Quoted in *Judaism*."
"By withdrawing into dialogue with God, man can attain the complete abandonment of his passions and evil habits..."

Scriptures that address conquering sin:

**Acts 3-26** "God raised up His Son to bless you, in turning away every one of you from his iniquities."

**1 Corinthians 15-57** "Whoever commits sin is a servant of sin, but thanks to God who gives us the victory through Jesus Christ, our Lord."

**Galatians 5-16** "Walk in the Spirit, and you will not fulfill the desires of the flesh

# PAUL'S EPISTLE TO THE ROMANS, CHAPTER 8
"Those guided by the Spirit are the sons of God."

**Romans 8-1 to 8-18** "There is therefore now no condemnation to those who walk after the Spirit. For the Spirit of life in Jesus has made me free from the law of sin and death. For what the law could not do, in that it was weak through the flesh, God sending His own Son... condemned sin in the flesh; that the righteousness (those moral aspects) of the Law are fulfilled in us who walk after the Holy Spirit. For they that are after the flesh mind the things of the flesh; but they who are after the Spirit, mind the things of the Spirit. But you are not in the flesh, but in the Spirit, if the Spirit of God dwells in you. Now if any man has not the Spirit of Christ, he is none of his. And if Christ is in you...the Spirit is life because of righteousness."

> Blaise Pascal, "Pensees"
> "It is the heart which experiences God and not the reason. This then is faith. Those to whom God has imparted Spiritual insight are very fortunate and justly convinced."

"If the Spirit of Him dwells in you, he shall also quicken your body by His Spirit that dwells in you. Therefore brethren if you, through the Spirit mortify the deeds of the body, you shall live.

For as many as are led by the Spirit of God, they are the sons of God. ... And if children then heirs; heirs of God, and joint heirs with Christ."

***Galatians 5-18, 22***: "If you are led by the Spirit, you are not under the 'Law'. The fruit of the Spirit is love, joy, peace, gentleness, goodness, faith, temperance... If we abide in the Spirit, let us also walk in the Spirit."

*Faith, if genuine, transcends into obedience which subsequently increases a person's faith because recognition builds with each Divine recommendation, exhortation or perhaps comforting thought. "Faith is evidence of the unseen." Experience provides the evidence; just as the natural world presents evidence of the Creator.*

<u>Beethoven</u> said to a friend one day, "I well know that God is nearer to me than others are. I commune with Him."

<u>K.B. Bamfield, "On Values"</u>
"I experience in myself in a manner which none other can teach me, the truth of the affirmation that God is."

<u>George Fox, "The Journal of George Fox"</u>
"I warned him to repent, and come to the Light with which Christ had enlightened him. That by it he might see all his evil words and actions, and turn to Christ Jesus while he had time, and that while he had time he should prize it. 'Ay, ay,' said he,
    'The Light that is spoken of in the third of John.' I desired he would mind it, and obey it."

**Romans 8-26, 27, 28** "Likewise the Spirit also helps our infirmities; for we know not what we should pray for as we ought, but the Spirit itself makes intercession for us, and He that searches the hearts knows what is the mind of the Spirit; for He makes intercession for the Saints... And we know that all things work together for good to those that love God; to those who are called according to His purpose."

<u>Francois Fenelon, "Spiritual Letters"</u>
"The word *Saint* means a man called out from among sinners, and in this sense all good men are saints."

**Romans 8:33-39** "Who shall lay anything to the charge of God's elect? It is God that justifies....Who shall separate us from the love of Christ? Shall tribulation or distress, or persecution, or famine, or nakedness, or peril, or sword? ..Nay in all these things we are more than conquerors through him that loved us. For I am persuaded that neither death, nor life, nor angels, nor principalities, nor powers, nor things present, nor things to come, nor height, nor depth, nor any other creature shall be able to separate us from the love of God, in Christ Jesus our Lord."

*"He makes intercession for the Saints." "He helps our infirmities." "The elect." "We are more than conquerors." "Who shall separate us from the love of God?"*
    A review of Romans 8-1 to 8-18 will determine if those Scriptures relate to one's own level of Spiritual growth that they may confidently claim for themselves the above oversights and protections. There are many Scriptures that admonish in various ways to, "walk worthy of the Lord." No one slips into His fold of acceptance the moment they state a *belief* or "*trust Jesus as Savior*." "The just (the upright) shall live by faith."

Robert Barclay:
"Whatsoever is excellent, whatsoever is noble, whatsoever is worthy, whatsoever is desirable in the Christian Faith, is ascribed to this Spirit; without which it could no more subsist than the outward world without the sun....It is not because it is ceased to become the privilege of every true Christian that they do not sense it, but rather because they are not so much Christians by nature as by name, and let such know that the secret light which shines in the heart, and reproves unrighteousness is the small beginning of the revelation of God's Spirit."

D.J. Mercier, "Conferences of..."
"How is it then, that the voice of God is not more distinctly heard by men? The answer to this question: To be heard it must be listened for."

<u>Harith IBN Asad Al-Muhasibi (850 A.D.)</u>
"Let him who wishes to be near to God, abandon all that alienates him from God."

<u>John Everard, "Spiritual Reformer."</u>
"If you turn the man loose who has found the living Guide within him, then let him neglect the outward if he can.

# Paul's Epistle to the Romans, Chapters 9 and 10

To his brethren, "Seek righteousness by faith. Faith comes by hearing."

It seems repetitive that Paul would, *as in Chapter 3*, issue the same plea to his brethren to seek justification by faith as opposed to adhering to their 'law for righteousness.' This Epistle is written exclusively to his brethren.

**Romans 9:1-4** "I say the truth in Christ, I lie not; my conscience also bearing me witness in the Holy Spirit, that I have great heaviness and continual sorrow in my heart. For I could wish that myself were accursed from Christ for my brethren, my kinsmen according to the flesh who are Israelites; to whom the adoption and the glory and the covenants, and the giving of the Law, and the promises...."

**9-30, 31, 32** "What shall we say then? That the Gentiles, who followed not after righteousness have attained to the righteousness which is of faith. But Israel, which followed after the law of righteousness hath not attained to the law of righteousness. Why? Because they sought it not by faith, but by the works of the law; they stumbled at that stumbling-stone."

**Romans 10:1-4** "Brethren, my heart's desire and prayer to God for Israel is that they might be saved. For I bear them record that they have a zeal for God, but not according to knowledge. Being ignorant of God's righteousness, (that of faith) and going about to establish their own righteousness, (by keeping the ordinances of their law) they have not submitted themselves unto the righteousness of God. For Christ is the end of the *Law* for righteousness to everyone that believes."

**Proverbs 15-9** "He loves him that follows after righteousness."

**Acts 10-35** "In every nation, he that fears [reverences] Him and works righteousness is acceptable with Him."

Stated sequentially and advancing from their 'Law' to 'Faith' and the ultimate 'walk in the Spirit,' the following Scriptures are from Paul's *Epistle to the Galatians* Chapters two through six:

1. "A person is not justified by the works of the law, but by the faith of Christ.
2. Did you receive the Spirit by the works of the law, or by the hearing of faith?
3. He that ministers to you the Spirit, and works miracles among you, does he do so by the works of the Law, or by the hearing of faith?
4. …That the blessing of Abraham might come to the Gentiles; that they might receive the promise of the Spirit through faith.
5. Had a law given life; righteousness would have been by the Law.
6. You observe days, and months and times and years. I am afraid of you, lest I have bestowed upon you labor in vain.
7. I travail in birth again until Christ be formed in you.
8. Stand fast therefore in the liberty wherewith Christ has made us free, and be not entangled again with the yoke of bondage.
9. Neither circumcision nor un-circumcision avails anything, but faith which works by love.
10. Walk in the Spirit, and you will not fulfill the desires of the flesh. If you are guided by the Spirit, you are not under the Law.
11. The fruit of the Spirit is love, joy, peace, longsuffering, gentleness, goodness, faith, temperance…
12. If we live in the Spirit, let us also walk in the Spirit; for sowing in the Spirit reaps Life Eternal."

<u>Continuing Romans Chapter 10:</u>
**10-8** "What does the word of faith say which we preach?
**10-9** "That if you shall confess with thy mouth the Lord Jesus, and shall believe in thy heart that God has raised him from the dead, thou shalt be saved."
**10-10** "For with the heart a person believes, unto righteousness."

It is important to keep in mind the sum of Chapter 6: Yielding to, or following righteousness, is serving God, with fruit unto holiness and the end, everlasting life.

The obvious conclusion for **10-10** is that 'believing' is not an indicator of righteousness forthcoming; nor is righteousness an outright gift, but Paul was addressing the Israelites who relied on the Law as their guide toward righteousness in order to gain approval from God. *Faith*, Paul hoped, would replace loyalty to their Law.

(Faith then advances to a Spiritual walk, as the above Galatian Scriptures describe.)

(Continuing Paul's letter to his brethren):
**Romans 10: 11, 12, 13** "For the scripture saith, whosoever believes on Him shall not be ashamed; for there is no difference between the Jew and the Greek. For the same Lord over all is rich unto all that call upon Him; for whosoever shall call upon the name of the Lord will be saved." [Indicating that no preference is made toward a Jew or a Greek when calling upon Him.]

"Not everyone who says Lord, Lord, will be saved, but those who do the will of my Father." (Being a generally good, upright and honest person can qualify for "doing His will."

**Romans 10: 14-21**
"How shall they call on Him in whom they have not believed, and how shall they believe on him in whom they have not heard, and how shall they hear without a preacher?

Have they not all heard? Yes, their sound went into all the earth, and their words to the end of the world. So then faith comes by hearing the word of God.

But they have not all obeyed the gospel. For Isaiah saith, 'Lord, who has believed our preaching'?

Isaiah is very bold and saith, 'I was found of them that sought me not; I was made manifest unto them that asked not after me.' But to Israel he saith, 'All day long I have stretched forth my hands to a disobedient and gainsaying people.'"

## Paul's Epistle to the Romans, chapter 11
Parable of the wild olive tree.

**Romans 11-1** "I say then has God cast away His people? God forbid, for I also am an Israelite, of the seed of Abraham, of the tribe of Benjamin...
**Romans 11-5** Even so then at this present time also there is a remnant according to the election of grace, and if by grace, then it is no more of works: otherwise grace is no more grace. But if it be of works, then is it no more grace; otherwise work is no more work."

> 'Works' of **11-5**, continues to refer to the Israelites' Law, (works of the law) and not to good works. This is evident for two reasons: (a) The negative connotation, and (b) he is referring to the Israelites. With **11-1**, the subject is a continuation from the two previous chapters.

**Romans 11-7, 11** "What then? Israel has not obtained that which he seeks for, but the election has obtained it, and the rest were blinded... Have they stumbled that they should fall? God forbid: but through their fall, salvation is unto the Gentiles for to provoke them to jealousy.
**Romans 11-13, 14** I speak to you Gentiles inasmuch as I am the apostle of the Gentiles, I magnify my office; if by any means I may provoke to emulation those of my flesh, and might save some of them.
**Romans 11-17 to 21** If some of the branches be broken off, and thou being a wild olive tree were grafted in among them;...boast not against the branches, but if thou boast, thou bear not the root, but the root thee. Because of unbelief they were broken off, and thou stands by faith. Be not high-minded, but fear. For if God spared not the natural branches, take heed lest he also spare not thee.
**Romans 11-22, 23** Behold therefore the goodness and severity of God: On them which fell, severity; but toward thee, goodness if thou

continue in *his*\* goodness; otherwise thou also shall be cut off. And they also, if they abide not still in unbelief, shall be grafted in: for God is able to graft them in again." (\* *'his'* may not have been in the original text as indicated by italics.)

# Paul's Epistle to the Romans, Chapters 12-16
## (A Brief Overview)
The importance of goodness and keeping the Commandments.
Love defined as, "working no ill toward others."

**Chapter 12**: "I beseech you therefore brethren, by the mercies of God, that you present your bodies a living sacrifice, holy and acceptable unto God. And be not conformed to the world, but be transformed that you may prove what is that good and acceptable and perfect will of God."

The importance of goodness noted throughout:
**12-9** "Abhor that which is evil; cleave to that which is good. Be kindly affectionate one to another...Be not slothful in business; provide things honest in the sight of all.
**12-21** Be not overcome of evil, but overcome evil with good.
**15-14** I am persuaded of you, brethren, that you also are full of goodness, filled with all knowledge, and able also to admonish one another.
**16-19** Your obedience is come abroad unto all. I would have you wise concerning that which is good, and harmless concerning evil."

**Chapter 13** "Owe no one anything, but to love one another: for he that loves another has fulfilled the Law. For this: 'Thou shalt not commit adultery, Thou shalt not kill, Thou shalt not steal, Thou shalt not bear false witness, Thou shalt not covet, and if there be any other Commandment, it is briefly comprehended in this saying, namely: Thou shalt love thy neighbor as thyself.' Love works no ill to his neighbor."

George Fox:
"Many 'Friends' [Quakers] that were tradesmen of several sorts, lost their customers at first, for the people were shy of them, and would not trade with them, so that for a time some 'Friends' could hardly get money enough to buy bread. But afterwards, when people came to have experience of 'Friends' honesty and

faithfulness; that they kept to a word in their dealings, and would not cozen and cheat, but if a child were sent to their shops for anything, he was as well-treated as his parents would have been.

Then the lives and conversation of 'Friends' did preach, and reached to the witness of God to the people. Then things altered so that all the inquiry was, 'where is there a draper, or a shop-keeper, or a tailor, or a shoemaker, or any other tradesman that is a Quaker?' In so much that 'Friends' had more trade than many of their neighbors, and if there was any trading, they had a great part of it. Then the envious professors altered their note, and began to cry out, 'If we let these Quakers alone, they will take the trade of the nation out of our hands.'"

**Chapter 14** "We shall all stand before the judgment seat of Christ. Every knee shall bow, and every tongue shall confess to God. So then every one of us shall give an account to God.

The Kingdom of God is not meat and drink, but righteousness and peace and joy in the Holy Spirit."

**Chapter 15** "Jesus was a minister of the circumcision for the truth; to confirm the promises unto the fathers, and that the Gentiles might glorify God; as it is written, 'For this cause I will confess to thee among the Gentiles, and sing unto thy name.' And again he says, 'Rejoice you Gentiles with his people.' And again, 'Praise the Lord, all you Gentiles…'"

"And again, Isaiah says, 'there shall be a root of Jesse that shall rise to reign over the Gentiles; in Him shall the Gentiles trust.'

Now may God fill you with joy and peace in believing, that you may abound in hope through the power of the Holy Spirit.

Because of the grace given to me of God, I should be the minister of Christ to the Gentiles, ministering the gospel of God that the offering up of the Gentiles might be acceptable; being sanctified by the Holy Spirit….

For I will not dare to speak of any of those things which Christ has not wrought by me to make the Gentiles obedient by word and deed."

**Chapter 16** "Mark them who cause divisions and offences contrary to the doctrine which you have learned, and avoid them. They serve not our Lord. By good words and fair speeches they deceive the hearts of the simple. Your obedience is come abroad unto all people. I would have you wise unto that which is good, and innocent concerning evil.

To Him that is of power to establish you according to my gospel, and by the scriptures of the prophets according to the Commandment of the everlasting God; made known to all nations for the obedience of faith:

To God only wise, be glory through Jesus Christ forever,"
Amen.

CHAPTER 5

# Paul's First Epistle to the Corinthians

~~

Our responsibility in Spiritual growth.

The two Epistles to the Corinthians and one to the Ephesians expound further on the subject of The Holy Spirit, as Romans, Chapter 8.

Paul's writing regarding 'our responsibility' is intermingled with the subject of the Holy Spirit as to be expected. The distinction is made here in both Corinthian letters; by singling out the message on our *responsibility* from the subject of *the Holy Spirit*, in order that one might appreciate more fully both intentions of Paul. (1 Corinthians chapter 13, is not included).

"Unto the Church of God which is at Corinth; to them that are sanctified in Christ Jesus, called saints.

Every man shall receive his own reward according to his own labor. I have begotten you through the gospel. Wherefore I beseech you, be you followers of me.

Know you not that the unrighteous shall not inherit the Kingdom of God? Be not deceived, neither fornicators, nor idolaters, nor adulterers, nor abusers of themselves with mankind, nor thieves, nor covetous, nor drunkards, nor revilers, nor extorters shall inherit the Kingdom of God. And such were some of you, but you are washed, but you are sanctified, but you are justified in the name of the Lord and by the Spirit of our God."

By the guidance of, and in cooperation with the Holy Spirit, "You are washed," as well as doing those things a person knows to do, the finer characteristics form and are rewarded with, "sanctification and justification."

**Hebrews 12-10** "He chastens us for our profit that we might be partakers of His Holiness."

"Know you not that they who run a race run all, but one receives the prize? So run that you may obtain. And every man that strives for the mastery is temperate in all things. Now they to obtain a corruptible crown, but we an incorruptible.
Wherefore let him who thinks that he stand; take heed lest he fall.
I preached unto you the gospel wherein you stand; by which also you are saved if you keep in memory what I preached unto you, unless you have believed in vain.
Awake to righteousness and sin not."

# Paul's First Epistle to the Corinthians
## The Spiritual Life

"To those who are sanctified in Christ Jesus, called saints: In everything you are enriched by him, in all utterance, and all knowledge.
  Of Him are you in Christ Jesus, who of God is made unto us wisdom, and righteousness, and sanctification and redemption."

> On "righteousness, sanctification and redemption," (Romans chapter 6): Following righteousness leads to holiness, (sanctification) onto everlasting life: (redemption)."

"My speech and preaching were in demonstration of the Spirit and power; that your faith should stand in the power of God.
  Eye has not seen, nor ear heard... what God has prepared for them that love Him, but He has revealed them unto us by His Spirit.
  We have received the Spirit of God that we might know the things freely given us of God. These things also we speak which the Holy Spirit teaches. Who has known the mind of the Lord, that He may instruct him? We have the mind of Christ.
  Know you not that you are the temple of God, and the Spirit of God dwells in you? I have begotten you through the Gospel; wherefore I beseech you, be followers of me.
  Your body is the temple of the Holy Spirit which you have of God, and you are not your own; you are bought with a price. Therefore glorify God in your body, and in your spirit which are His.
  There are diversities of operation, but the same God works all and in all. For to one is given by the Spirit, the word of wisdom; to another the word of knowledge by the same Spirit; to another, faith by the same Spirit; to another the gifts of healing; to another the working of miracles; to another prophecy; to another the discerning of spirits.

The sting of death is sin, but thanks to God who gives us the victory through our Lord. Therefore be you steadfast, always abounding in the work of the Lord, forasmuch as you know that your labor is not in vain in the Lord...Stand fast in the faith. ... like men, be strong."

# Paul's Second Epistle to the Corinthians
Our responsibility in Spiritual growth.

"Unto the Church of God which is at Corinth with all the saints in Achaia.

We have renounced the hidden things of dishonesty, not walking in craftiness, not handling the word of God deceitfully…commending ourselves to every man's conscience in the sight of God.

We labor… that we may be accepted of Him, for we must all appear before the judgment seat of Christ; that everyone may receive according to the things that he has done, whether good or bad. Knowing therefore the terror of the Lord, we persuade men, but we are made manifest unto God, and I trust also are made manifest in your consciences.

Be not unequally yoked together with unbelievers; for what fellowship has righteousness with unrighteousness, and what communion has light with darkness?

You are the temple of God, as He has said, "And I will dwell in them and walk in them….

Having therefore these promises, dearly beloved, let us cleanse ourselves from all filthiness of flesh and spirit, perfecting holiness in the fear of God.

Though I made you sorry with a letter, I do not repent. Now I rejoice, not that you were made sorry, but that you sorrowed to repentance; for godly sorrow works repentance to salvation.

As you abound in everything, in faith, and utterance and knowledge, and in all diligence, I speak to prove the sincerity of your love…

For you know the grace of our Lord Jesus; that though he was rich, yet for your sakes he became poor; that you through his poverty might be rich…

Now therefore perform the doing of it; that as there was a readiness to will, so there be a performance also out of that which you have.

He who sows sparingly shall reap also sparingly; and he that sows bountifully shall reap also bountifully. You always, having all sufficiency in all, may abound to every good work. As it is written, 'He hath given to the poor; his righteousness remains forever.'

Not he that commends himself is approved, but whom the Lord commends.

I fear, when I come I shall find debates, envying, wraths, strife, backbiting, whisperings, tumults… Examine yourselves, whether you are in the faith; test your own selves. Know you not your own selves, how that Jesus is in you, except you be reprobates?

## <u>Paul's Second Epistle to the Corinthians</u>
The Spiritual Life

"Now He who establishes us with you in Christ, and has anointed us, is God; who has also sealed us, and given the earnest of the Spirit in our hearts.

You are our epistle written in our hearts, known and read of all men; written not with ink, but with the Spirit of the Living God in the tables of the heart.

Our sufficiency is of God who has made us able ministers of the New Testament; not of the letter, but of the Spirit. The Spirit gives life. Now the Lord is that Spirit; and where the Spirit of the Lord is, there is liberty.

We all with open face beholding as in a glass the Glory of the Lord, are changed into the same image by the Spirit of the Lord.

God, who commanded the light to shine out of darkness, has shined in our hearts to give the light of the knowledge of God in the face of Jesus.

If anyone is in Christ, he is a new creature. Old things have passed away. All things have become new.

In all things approve ourselves as the ministers of God…by pureness, by knowledge, by longsuffering, by kindness, by the Holy Spirit, by love unfeigned, by the word of truth, by the power of God, by the armor of righteousness.

You are the temple of the Living God, as God as said: I will dwell in them, and walk in them, and I shall be their God, and they will be my people."

## John Milton.

"In his mind itself there were purity and piety absolute; an imagination to which neither the past nor the present were interesting, except as far as they called forth and enlivened the great ideal, in which and for which he lived: a keen love of truth; which after many weary pursuits, found a harbor in a sublime listening to the still voice in his own spirit. Also as keen a love of his country, which after a disappointment still more depressive, expanded and soared into a love of mankind. These were; these alone could be the conditions under which such work as the *Paradise Lost* could be conceived and accomplished."
　　　　　Samuel T. Coleridge, "Aids to Reflection"

"And chiefly thou O Spirit, that dost prefer
Before all temples, th' upright heart and pure.
Instruct me, for Thou know'st, Thou from the first
Was present: what in me is dark illumine,
What is low raise and support;
That…I may assert eternal Providence,
And justify the ways of God to man.
　　　John Milton, "Paradise Lost," Book 1: (Introductory)

"Obedience to the Spirit of God, rather than to the fair seeming pretense of men, is the best and most dutiful order that a Christian can observe." John Milton, 1642.

## Paul's Epistle to the Ephesians
A poignant correspondence to the Gentile-Christians.

The only letter written exclusively to the Gentiles. His ardent hope for their Spiritual progress is a tender-hearted appeal beginning with Chapter 2 vs.18.

**Ephesians 1-13** (A summary) "To the saints who are at Ephesus, and to the faithful in Christ Jesus. According as he has chosen us in Him before the foundation of the world; that we should be holy and without blame before him in love…He has abounded toward us in all wisdom and all prudence having made known unto us the mystery of His will according to his good pleasure. We should be to the praise of his glory, who first trusted in Christ…In whom you also after you heard the word of truth, the gospel of your salvation: in whom also after you believed you were sealed with the Holy Spirit."

**1 Corinthians 15-1, 2** I declared unto you the Gospel wherein you stand, by which also you are saved if you hold fast what I preached unto you, unless you have believed in vain.

**Ephesians 1-16, 19** I give thanks for you making mention of you in my prayers that the God of our Lord may give unto you the spirit of wisdom and revelation in the knowledge of Him. The eyes of your understanding being enlightened; that you may know…the exceeding greatness of His power to us-ward who believe.
**Ephesians 2-8, 9, 10** For by grace are you saved through faith; and that not of yourselves, it is the gift of God; not of works [of the Law] lest any man should boast, for we are his workmanship created unto good works, which God has before ordained that we should walk in them.
**Ephesians 2:11-16** …Wherefore remember that you in time past, Gentiles in the flesh who are called uncircumcision by the circumcision; that at that time you were without Christ, being aliens from the

commonwealth of Israel, and strangers from the covenants of promise... without God in the world. But now in Christ Jesus you who sometimes were far off are made nigh by the blood of Christ. For he is our peace, who has made both one, and has broken down the middle wall of partition; having abolished in his flesh the enmity, the law of commandments in ordinances for to make in himself of twain, one new man, and that he might reconcile both unto God in one body by the cross, having slain the enmity thereby, and came and preached peace to you who were afar off, and to them that were nigh..."

<u>Ephesians,</u> beginning with Chapter 2 vs.18.
"We both, Jew and Gentile have access by one Spirit unto the Father. The building, fitly-framed together, grows unto a holy Temple for a habitation of God through the Spirit.

I bow my knees unto the Father that He would grant you to be strengthened with might by His Spirit in the inner person. That Christ may dwell in your hearts by faith; that you being rooted and grounded in love may be able to comprehend with all saints, what is the breadth, the length, the depth and height, and to know the love of Christ.

I beseech you to walk worthy of the vocation wherewith you are called.

He gave some apostles, some teachers for the perfecting of the saints till we all come unto a perfect person, unto the measure of the stature of the fullness of Christ. Be no more children tossed to and fro with every wind of doctrine, but speaking the truth, grow up unto Him in all things."

"Walk not as other Gentiles in the vanity of the mind having their understanding darkened; alienated from the life of God because of the blindness of their heart. Who being past feeling have given themselves over to lasciviousness.

You are not so, learned Christ if that you have heard Him and been taught by him. Put on the new person who is created in righteousness and true holiness. Put aside malice, wrath, stealing, lying, clamor, evil speaking; for no unclean person has any inheritance in the Kingdom of God. Grieve not the Holy Spirit.

Walk as children of light; for the fruit of the Spirit is in all goodness and righteousness and truth, proving what is acceptable to the Lord. Walk circumspectly as the wise, understanding what the will of the Lord is.

Take on the breastplate of righteousness."

# Paul's First Epistle to Timothy
"Be an example to believers."

"Paul, an Apostle of Jesus Christ by the Commandment of our God: unto Timothy, my own son in the faith. Now the end of the Commandment is charity out of a pure heart, and a good conscience and genuine faith.

I thank God who hath enabled me; for He counted me faithful putting me into the ministry who was before a blasphemer, and a persecutor, and injurious, but I obtained mercy, because I did so ignorantly in unbelief. This is a faithful saying and worthy of all acceptation, that Christ came into the world to save sinners; of whom I am chief.

I commit unto thee, son Timothy… that thou hold faith, and a good conscience; which some having put away concerning faith have made shipwreck. Lead a quiet and peaceable life in all godliness and honesty; for this is good and acceptable to God who would have everyone saved, and come to the knowledge of the truth.

Now the Spirit speaks expressly, that in the latter times some shall depart from the faith, giving heed to seducing spirits and doctrines of devils.

Bodily exercise profits for a little time, but godliness is profitable unto all things; having promise of the life that now is, and of that which is to come.

Let no man despise thy youth; but be thou an example of the believers in word, in conversation, in charity, in spirit, in faith and in purity… Give attendance to reading… Take heed unto thyself, in continuing the doctrine; thou shalt both save thyself, and them that hear thee."

<u>Samuel T. Coleridge, "Aids to Reflection".</u>
"It is worthy of especial observation, that the Scriptures are distinguished from all other writings…by the strong and frequent recommendations of knowledge, and a spirit of inquiry."

Follow after righteousness, godliness, faith, love, patience, gentleness; laying hold on eternal life whereunto thou art also called.

Charge them that are rich in this world; that they… trust not in uncertain riches… That they do good, are rich in good works, ready to distribute, willing to communicate; laying up for themselves a good foundation… that they may lay hold on eternal life."

<u>Alexis De Tocqueville: "Democracy in America."</u>
"Men cannot be cured of the love of riches; but they may be persuaded to enrich themselves by none but honest means."

Paul's concern for Timothy's salvation is exemplary.

1. "Live in godliness and honesty, for this is good and acceptable to God <u>who would have all to be saved.</u>
2. Godliness has the promise of <u>the life which is to come</u>.
3. Be an example of the believers in word, charity, purity, conversation and in doctrine; <u>to save thyself, and them that hear thee.</u>
4. Follow after righteousness, faith, love, patience, gentleness; <u>laying hold on eternal life.</u>

# Paul's Epistle to the Hebrews
## The Provocation.

**Hebrews chapter 3: 10-15** "Wherefore, as the Holy Spirit saith, 'Today if you will hear His voice, harden not your hearts, as in *The Provocation*, the day of temptation in the wilderness when your fathers tempted me and saw my works for forty years. Wherefore I was grieved with that generation, and said, 'They do always err in their heart.' So I swore in my wrath, they shall not enter into my rest. Take heed brethren, lest there be in any of you an evil heart of unbelief, in departing from the living God...While it is said, 'Today, if you will hear His voice, harden not your hearts, as in the Provocation.'"

<u>An Old Testament study of the Israelites' conduct during the 'wilderness' years forming the basis for their being denied: His 'Rest':</u>

**Exodus 19-5** "You have seen how I bore you on Eagles wings, and brought you unto myself; now therefore, if you will obey my voice and keep my covenant, then you shall be a peculiar treasure unto me above all people...."

**Exodus 24-7** "And he took the book of the covenant, and read it to the people: and they said, "All that the Lord has said, will we do and be obedient.""

**Deuteronomy 1: 31-35** "In the wilderness, where thou hast seen that the Lord thy God bare thee, as a man doth bear his son, until you came into this place; yet in this thing you did not believe the Lord your God who went in the way before you to search you out a place to pitch your tents: in fire by night to show you the way you should go, and in a cloud by day. The Lord heard the voice of your words, and was wroth, and swore saying, 'surely there shall not one of these men of this evil generation see that good land.'"

**Deuteronomy 4-30** "If thou turn to the Lord thy God, and shall be obedient unto His voice, He will not forsake thee."

**Deuteronomy 27-10** "Thou shalt therefore obey the voice of the Lord thy God, and do His Commandments and His Statutes."

**Psalm 95-7, 10, 11** "We are the people of His pasture, and the sheep of His hand. Today if you will hear His voice, harden not your hearts as in the Provocation.... 'For 40 years long was I grieved with this generation, and said, it is a people that do err in their heart…Unto whom I swore in my wrath that they should not enter into my rest.'"

**Psalm 106-11, 12, 13, 24** "The waters covered their enemies; there was not one of them left. Then believed they His words; they sang His praise. They soon forgot His works; they waited not for His counsel, but sinned exceedingly in the wilderness. Yea, they despised the pleasant land; they believed not His word, but murmured in their tents, and hearkened not unto the voice of the Lord."

**Numbers 14-22** "And they have not hearkened to my voice; surely they shall not see the land promised to their fathers, neither shall any of them that provoked me see it, but Caleb because he had another spirit with him, and has followed me fully."

New Testament on The Provocation:
**1 Corinthians 10** "Moreover, brethren, I would not that you should be ignorant, how that all our fathers were under the cloud, and all passed through the sea… but with many of them God was not well pleased; for they were overthrown in the wilderness.

Now these things were our examples to the intent we should not lust after evil things, as they also lusted. In one day fell three and twenty thousand. Neither be idolaters as some of them, nor fornicators…Now all these things are written for our admonition… Wherefore let him that thinks he stands, take heed lest he fall."

<u>Hebrews 4-1, 2</u> "Let us therefore fear, lest a promise being left of entering into His 'rest', any of you should seem to come short of it. For unto us was the gospel preached, as well as unto them, but the word preached did not profit them, not being mixed with faith in them that heard it.
<u>Hebrews 4-3</u> For we who have believed do enter into rest. (Referring to the peaching of the gospel.)
<u>Hebrews 4-10</u> …For he that is entered into His rest, also has ceased from his own works, as God did from His."

Scriptures in this Epistle on good works:

**6-10** "God…will not forget you work and labor of love."
**10-24** "And let us consider one another to encourage unto love and to good works."
**13-21** "May the God of peace…make you perfect in every good work to do His will."

<u>Hebrews 4-11</u> "Let us labor therefore to enter into that rest; lest anyone fall after the same example of unbelief."

**The Key Point**: The optional word in King James Version for *unbelief* noted in the margin for verse **4-11**, is *disobedience*, which describes more accurately than *unbelief*, the conduct of the Israelites during "the wilderness years."

No longer is it valid to boast, "We believe, therefore we can enter into His rest!"

CHAPTER 6

# The Epistle of James

"Be doers of the word, not hearers only."

"JAMES, A SERVANT OF GOD and of the Lord Jesus: to the twelve tribes which are scattered abroad.

Be doers of the word and not hearers only, deceiving yourselves. For if any be a hearer of the word, and not a doer, he is like a man beholding his natural face in a glass; for straightway he forgets what manner of man he was. But whoso continues therein, he being not a forgetful hearer, but a doer of the work, this person shall be blessed in his deed.

Anyone who seems to be religious, and bridles not his tongue, deceives his own heart; this man's religion is vain. Pure religion and undefiled before God and the Father is this: to visit the fatherless and widows in their affliction, and to keep oneself unspotted from the world.

If you fulfill the royal law according to the Scripture, Thou shalt love thy neighbor as thyself, you do well... What does it profit, my brethren, though a person says he has faith, and has not works? Can faith save him? If a brother or sister be naked and destitute of daily food, and one of you say to them to 'depart in peace, be warmed and filled,' yet give them not those things needful to the body; even so then faith, if it hath not works is dead, being alone.

Yea, a person may say, 'Thou has faith, and I have works. Show me thy faith without thy works, and I will show thee my faith *by* my works.'

You believe that there is one God. You do well: the devils also believe and tremble.

But wilt thou know, O vain man that faith without works is dead?

Was not Abraham our father justified by works when he obeyed God and offered Isaac upon the altar?"

See thou how faith wrought with his works, and by works was faith made perfect? And the Scripture was fulfilled which said, 'Abraham believed God, and it was imputed unto him for righteousness, and he was called the Friend of God.' You see then how that by works a man is justified and not by faith only.

Likewise also was not Rahab... justified by works when she had received the messengers, and sent them another way? For as the body without the spirit is dead, so faith without works is dead also."

The tongue is a little member and boasts great things. Behold how great a matter a little fire kindles. The tongue can no man tame; it is an unruly evil full of deadly poison....Out of the same mouth proceeds blessing and cursing. My brethren, these things ought not to be. Does a fountain send forth at the same place, sweet and bitter water?"

<u>John Stott, "Basic Christianity:"</u>
"...Sometimes, it must be confessed with shame; others who make no Christian profession, seem to show more compassion than we who claim to know Christ."

Who is a wise person endued with knowledge among you? Let him show out of a good conduct his works. The wisdom that is from above is first pure, then peaceable, gentle, easy to be entreated, full of mercy and good fruits; without wrangling, and without hypocrisy.

Submit yourselves to God. Draw near to God, and He will draw near to you. Purify you heart. Humble yourselves in the sight of the Lord, and He will lift you up. To him that knows to do right, and does it not, it is sin. Establish your hearts, for the coming of the Lord draws nigh.

Is any among you afflicted? Let him pray. Is any merry? Let him sing psalms.

The effectual fervent prayer of a righteous person avails much.

Brethren, if any of you do err from the truth, and one convert him, let him know that he which converts the sinner from the error of his way, shall save a soul from death, and shall hide a multitude of sins."

# The Second Epistle of Peter
*Righteousness:* "Be diligent to be found blameless."

**2 Peter 1-1** …"To them that have obtained like precious faith with us through the righteousness of God."

**2 Peter 1: 3-11** "According as His Divine power hath given unto us all things that pertain to life and godliness… Whereby are given unto us exceeding great and precious promises: that by these you might be partakers of the Divine Nature. …Giving all diligence, add to your faith, virtue; and to virtue, knowledge; and to knowledge, temperance and to temperance, patience. Add to patience, godliness, and to godliness, kindness, and to kindness, charity. For if these things are in you and abound, you shall neither be barren nor unfruitful. If you do these things, you shall never fall: for so an entrance shall be ministered unto you into the everlasting Kingdom of our Lord and Savior, Jesus Christ.

We made known unto you the power and coming of our Lord. We were eyewitnesses of His Majesty; for He received from God the Father, honor and glory when there came such a voice to Him from glory, 'This is my beloved Son in whom I am well pleased.' And this Voice which came from Heaven we heard when we were with him in the Holy Mount."

**2 Peter Chapters 2 and 3** "God spared not the old world, but saved Noah, a preacher of righteousness, bringing the flood upon the world of the ungodly, and turning the cities of Sodom and Gomorrah into ashes-- condemned with an overthrow; making an example unto those that after should live ungodly. He delivered upright Lot who was vexed with the filthy conversation of the wicked.

The Lord knows how to deliver the godly out of temptation. The unjust that walk after the flesh shall receive the reward of unrighteousness… They have forsaken the right way and are gone astray. These are wells without water…

The Lord is not slack concerning His promise, but is longsuffering to us; not willing that any should perish, but that all should come to repentance. The day of the Lord will come as a thief in the night in which the heavens will pass away with a great noise, and the elements will melt with fervent heat. The earth also and the works therein will be burned up.

Seeing then that all these things shall be dissolved, what manner of persons ought you to be in all holy conversation and godliness .

Nevertheless we, according to His promise, look for the new Heavens and a new Earth wherein dwells righteousness. Wherefore, beloved, seeing that you look for such things, be diligent that you may be found of him in peace… and blameless."

"…And account that the long-suffering of our Lord is salvation; as our beloved brother Paul also according to the wisdom given to him has written to you; as also in all of his epistles speaking of these things in which are some things hard to be understood.

Seeing you know, beware lest you also, being led away with the error of the wicked, fall from your own steadfastness…."

<u>Other Scripture references on the End Time:</u>

**Matthew 24-31, 44** "And he shall send his angels with a great sound of a trumpet, and they shall gather together his elect from the four winds, from one end of Heaven to the other. Therefore be you also ready; for in such an hour as you think not, the Son of man comes."

**Luke 21-36** "Watch you therefore, and pray always, that you may be accounted worthy to escape all these things that shall come to pass, and to stand before the Son of Man."

**John 5-28, 29** "All that are in the graves shall hear His voice, and shall come forth. Those who have done good unto the resurrection of life."

**Thessalonians 4-16, 17, 21, 23**: "The Lord shall descend with a shout...and the dead in Christ shall rise first...then we who are alive...shall be caught up together with them in the clouds to meet the Lord in the air...Prove all things; hold fast that which is good. I pray your whole spirit and soul and body be preserved blameless unto the coming of our Lord."

**James 5-8** "Establish your hearts for the coming of the Lord draws nigh."

Marcus Aurelius, "Meditations"
"But, my good friend, consider whether nobility and goodness are not something different from saving and being saved."

"There is no respect of persons with God."

**Acts 10-35** "Of a truth I perceive that God is no respecter of persons; but in every nation he that fears [reverences] Him and works righteousness is acceptable to Him."

**Romans 2: 6-11** "He will render to every man according to his deeds: To them who continue in well-doing... eternal life, but unto them who obey unrighteousness; indignation and wrath... To the Jew first and also the Gentile: For there is no respect of persons with God."

**Ephesians 6-8, 9** "Whatsoever good thing a person does, the same shall he receive of the Lord; for there is no respect of persons with God."

**Colossians 3-25** "He that does wrong shall receive for the wrong he has done, and there is no respect of persons with God."

**1 Peter 1-17** "Without respect of persons, He judges according to every man's work."

# THE FIRST EPISTLE OF JOHN, CHAPTERS 1-4
"He that says he abides in Him, ought to walk as He walked."

"That which was from the beginning which we have heard, we have seen with our eyes…That which we have seen and heard, we write unto you. We are of God. He that knows God, hears us.

If we say that we have fellowship with Him, and walk in darkness, we do not tell the truth. But if we walk in the light, as he is in the light, we have fellowship one with another, and we are cleansed from all sin. If we say that we have no sin, we lie. If we confess our sins, he is faithful and just to forgive us and to cleanse us from all unrighteousness."

"If we say we have no sin, we lie…." Often interpreted as, 'We are human; therefore we are subject to sin. Confessing the sin however, leads to forgiveness and a 'cleansing from all unrighteousness."

Looking closer at the above: "…if we walk in the light, as He is in the light…we are cleansed from all sin." The difference is in the 'walk' compared to the average person who claims susceptibility to sin, with forgiveness, the remedy.

As this first Epistle of John continues, it becomes quite clear that he does not accept sin as an inevitable human susceptibility.

"We know that we know Him if we keep His commandments. He that says, 'I know Him,' and keeps not His commandments, the truth is not in him. But whosoever keeps His word, in him verily is the love of God perfected; hereby know we that we are in him. He that says he abides in him ought also to walk, even as he walked. He that loves his brother abides in the light.

The anointing which you have received of him abides in you, and you need not that anyone teach you, but as the same anointing teaches you, you shall abide in him…and when he shall appear, we may have confidence before him at his coming. If you know that he is righteous, you know that everyone that does righteousness is born of God.

Beloved now are we the sons of God. We know that when he shall appear, we shall be like him, and every man that has this hope purifies himself... Whosoever commits sin, transgresses the Law. And you know that he was manifested to take away our sins. Whosoever abides in him, sins not. Whosoever sins has not seen him, neither known him. Let no man deceive you: he that does righteousness is righteous, as He is righteous. He that commits sin is of the devil. Whoever is born of God does not commit sin."

"Let us not love in word, neither in tongue, but in deed and in truth. Hereby we know that we are of the truth, and shall assure our hearts before Him; for if our heart condemn us, God is greater than our heart, and knows all things. If our heart condemn us not, then we have confidence toward God, and whatsoever we ask, we receive of him, because we keep His Commandments, and do those things that are pleasing in His sight."

"And this is His Commandment: That we should believe on the name of his Son, Jesus Christ, and love one another as he gave us commandment. And he that keeps his Commandments dwells in him, and he in him. And hereby we know that he abides in us, by the Spirit which He has given us."

## The First Epistle of John, Chapter 5
Scriptures that augment believing.

The following Scriptures, in 1 John Chapter 5 seem to slight other responsibilities that accompany an active faith, as expounded on throughout the New Testament including the first four chapters of this, John's first Epistle.

The Apostles Paul, James, Peter, John and the Gospels have covered thoroughly the subject of salvation, and the unanimous agreement is that everyone must follow the good, and avoid wrongdoing.

By drawing on relevant Scriptures, an attempt is made to clarify those in Chapter 5 which imply that 'believing' meets all requirements for salvation.

**1 JOHN 5-1 and 5-5**: "Whosoever believes that Jesus is the Christ is born of God. Who is he that overcomes the world, but he that believes that Jesus is the Son of God."

<u>1 John 2-29</u> "If you know that He is righteous, know you also that everyone that does righteousness is born of God."

<u>1 John 3-9</u> "Whosoever is born of God does not commit sin."

**I JOHN 5-10, 11** "He that believes on the Son of God has this witness in himself: This is the record that God has given us: eternal life, and this life is in His Son.

<u>1 John 1-6</u> "If we say we have fellowship with Him, and walk in darkness, we do not tell the truth".

<u>1 John 2-6</u> "Whosoever says he abides in him ought also to walk, even as he walked."

**1 John 5-13** "These things have I written to you that believe on the name of the Son of God; that you may know that you have eternal life."

<u>John 2-17</u> "The world passes away, but he that does the will of God abides forever."

<u>1 John 2-5</u> "Whosoever keeps his word, in him verily is the love of God perfected."

# The Second and Third Epistles of John
## The 'walk' and the 'good.'

**2 John 6** …"And this is love; that we walk after His Commandments. This is the Commandment, that which you have heard from the beginning, you should walk therein.

**3 John 11** Beloved, follow not that which is evil, but that which is good. He that does good is of God, but he that does evil hath not seen God.

CHAPTER 7

# Biographical

"Though thy beginning was small, yet thy latter end should greatly increase; for inquire, I pray thee of the former age, and prepare thyself for the search of the fathers...Shall not they teach thee, and tell thee, and utter words out of their heart?"

The Book of Job 8: 7, 8, 10.

# SOCRATES

"Socrates was born in Athens in 470 B.C. He was the first to teach ethics systemically from principles of moral obligation. He was a profoundly religious man, recognized Providence, and believed in the immortality of the soul. He deduced the existence of God from the order and harmony of nature. He endeavored to connect the moral with the religious consciousness and thus to promote the practical welfare of society. In this light Socrates stands out the grandest personage of pagan antiquity—as a moralist, as a teacher of ethics, as a man who recognized the Divine."

By John Lord

"The indictment runs thus: 'Meletus says that Socrates is an evil-doer who corrupts the youth, and he does not believe in the gods whom the city believes in, but in other new divinities.'"

Socrates:
"I ought never to have been brought to trial at all, and that as it is, you are bound to put me to death, because as he said if I escape, all your children will forthwith be utterly corrupted by practicing what Socrates teaches. If you were therefore to say to me, 'Socrates, this time we will not listen to Anytus; we will let you go; but on this condition: that you cease from carrying on this search of yours'...I should reply...'Athenians, I hold you in the highest regard and love, but I will obey God rather than you: and as long as I have breath and strength I will not cease from philosophy, and from exhorting you, and declaring the truth to every one of you whom I meet, saying as I am wont, My excellent friend, you are a citizen of Athens, a city which is very great and very famous for wisdom and power of mind. Are you not ashamed of caring so much for the making of money,

and for reputation, and for honor? Will you not think or care about wisdom, and truth, and the perfection of your soul?' ...This I shall do to everyone whom I meet, young or old, citizen or stranger; but more especially to the citizens, for they are more nearly akin to me. For know well, God has commanded me to do so. And I think that no better piece of fortune has ever befallen you in Athens, than my service to God. For I spend my whole life in going about and persuading you all to give your first and chiefest care to the perfection of your souls, and not till you have done that; to think of your bodies, or your wealth, and telling you that virtue does not come from wealth, but that wealth, and every other good thing which men have, whether in public, or in private comes from virtue. If then I corrupt the youth by this teaching, the mischief is great; but if any man says that I teach anything else, he speaks falsely.

Either acquit me, or do not acquit me: but be sure that I shall not alter my way of life; no, not if I have to die for it many times....

I am trying to persuade you not to sin against God by condemning me and rejecting His gift to you. For if you put me to death you will not easily find another man to fill my place. God has sent me to attack the city as if it were a great and noble horse, to use a quaint simile, which was rather sluggish from its size, and which needed to be aroused by a gadfly, and I think that I am the gadfly that God has sent to the city to attack it, for I never cease from settling upon you, as it were at every point, and rousing and exhorting and reproaching each man of you all day long....

And you may easily see that it is God who has given me to your city. A mere human impulse would never have led me to neglect all my own interests, or to endure seeing my private affairs neglected now for so many years, while it made me busy myself unceasingly in your interests, and go to each man of you by himself, like a father, or an elder brother, trying to persuade him to care for virtue. There would have been a reason for it, if I had gained any advantage by this conduct, or if I had been paid for my exhortations.

I have a certain divine sign from God, which is the divinity that Meletus has caricatured in his indictment. I have had it from childhood: it is a kind of voice which whenever I hear it, always turns me back from something which I was going to do, but never urges me to act. It is this which forbids me to take part in politics. And I think that it does well to forbid me; for Athenians, it is quite certain that if I had attempted to take part in politics, I should have perished at once and long ago, without doing any good either to you or to myself. And do not be vexed with me for telling the truth."

(Socrates is condemned to die.)

I think that it is a much harder thing to escape from wickedness than from death; for wickedness is swifter than death. My accusers who are clever and swift, have been overtaken by the swifter pursuer, which is wickedness. And now I shall go hence, sentenced by you to death, and they will go hence, sentenced by truth to receive the penalty of wickedness....

And now I wish to prophesy to you, Athenians, who have condemned me; for I am going to die, and that is the time when men have most prophetic power. I prophesy to you who have sentenced me to death, that a far severer punishment than you have inflicted on me will surely overtake you as soon as I am dead. You have done this thing thinking that you will be relieved from having to give an account of your lives. But I say that the result will be very different from that.

The prophetic sign which I am wont to receive from the Divine Voice, has been constantly with me all through my life till now, opposing me in quite small matters if I were not going to act rightly...The sign of God did not withstand me when I was leaving my house this morning; nor when I was coming up hither to the Court, nor at any point in my speech when I was going to say anything; though at other times, it has often stopped me in the very act of speaking. This thing that has come upon me must be a good, and those of us who think that death is an evil must needs be mistaken. I have a clear proof that that is so, for my accustomed sign would certainly have opposed me, if I had not been going to fare well."

Minutes before his execution, Socrates said, "I say, let a man be of good cheer about his soul. When the soul has been arrayed in her own proper jewels: temperance and justice and courage, and nobility and truth—she is ready to go on her journey when the hour comes."

"The Apology of Socrates" from *The Dialogues of Plato*.
(Final paragraph from Plato's *Phaedo*).

## Clement of Alexandria

"He was one of the first great names in the famous "Christian Training School" of Alexandria for training young Christians…It was of inestimable importance for the transformation of the heathen empire into a Christian one, and for the transformation of Greek Philosophy into Christian Philosophy. It was largely through the work of the great teachers who came in succession in this school, that Christianity was made a part of the thought and civilization of the ancient world. He became a teacher in the school about 180 A.D.

His writings include, "An Address to the Greeks." The treatise undertakes to prove the superiority of Christianity to the religion and philosophy of the pagan world. In it he wrote: 'A noble hymn of God is an immortal man established in righteousness with truth engraved in his heart.'

Truth for him, by whomever spoken is from God… 'God as Spirit, moving through all life, and in immediate relation with the souls of people,' is fundamental to Clement's thought.

What the Law was for the Hebrews, philosophy was for the Greeks. 'Before the coming of the Lord,' he says, 'Philosophy was necessary to the Greeks for righteousness.' Clement calls the man of knowledge… who has the vision of God and holds communion with Him: 'The harmonized man.'"

[In Clement's words]:

"Doing good consists in the habit of doing good; not for glory, nor for reputation, nor for reward, either from men or God—but to be like the Lord."

"Faith grows with the exercise of obedience and becomes a kind of Divine mutual and reciprocal correspondence."

"There is no schism between faith and works, for faith is the beginning of action…" "Prayer is inward converse with God. The aim of Prayer is not to get things that are good, but to be good and to attain the habit of goodness…"

Rufus Jones, "The Luminous Trail."

## St. Augustine (353-430)

"The most intellectual of all the Fathers of the Church was doubtless Saint Augustine. He directed the thinking of the Christian world for a thousand years. He was more original than any of the great lights who shed the radiance of genius on the crumbling fabric of the ancient civilization. He is the sainted doctor of the church, equally an authority with both Catholics and Protestants…His humanity, his breadth, his charity, and his piety have endeared him to the heart of the Christian world.

Augustine was born near Carthage, in the Numidian province of the Roman Empire in the year A.D. 353. His parentage was humble…his father was a heathen, and lived, as Augustine tells us, in 'heathenish sin,' but his mother was a woman of remarkable piety and strength of mind; devoted to the education of her son. Augustine never alludes to her except with veneration, and his history adds additional confirmation to the fact that nearly all the remarkable men of our world have had remarkable mothers. Monica had an intense solicitude for his Spiritual interests, and her extraordinary faith in his future conversion in spite of his youthful follies and excesses; was encouraged by that good bishop who told her, 'It is impossible that the child of so many prayers could be lost….'

Augustine, in his 'Confessions,' that remarkable book which has lasted 1500 years and is still prized for its intensity, its candor and its profound acquaintance with the human heart; as well as evangelical truth; …tells us that until he was sixteen he was obstinate, lazy, neglectful of his studies, indifferent to reproach, and abandoned to heathenish sports. He even committed petty thefts, was quarrelsome, and indulged in demoralizing pleasures. At nineteen he was sent to Carthage to be educated, where he went still further astray; was a follower of stage-players, and gave himself up to unholy loves. But his intellect was inquiring, his nature genial and his habits as studious as could be reconciled with a life of pleasure… He seemed at an early age to be a sincere inquirer after truth.

His great abilities were seen and admired so that when the people of Milan sent to Symachus, the prefect of the city, to procure for them an able teacher of rhetoric, he sent Augustine,---a Providential matter; since in the second capital of Italy he heard the great Ambrose preach. He found one Christian whom he respected, whom he admired, and him he sought...At first Augustine listened as a critic, trying the eloquence of Ambrose, whether it answered the fame thereof, or flowed fuller or lower than was reported. 'But, of the matter I was,' says Augustine, 'a scornful and careless looker on; being delighted with the sweetness of his discourse. Yet I was, though by little and little, gradually drawing nearer and nearer to truth; for though I took no pains to learn *what* he spoke, only to hear *how* he spoke. And while I opened my heart to admire how eloquently he spoke, I also felt how truly he spoke. And so by degrees I resolved to abandon forever the Manicheans whose falsehoods I detested, and determined to be a catechumen of the Catholic Church.'

This was the great crisis of his life. He had renounced a false philosophy; he sought truth from a Christian bishop putting himself under Christian influences. It was not easy to overcome the loose habits of his life. Sensuality ever robs a man of the power of will. He had a double nature: a strong sensual from his sins...The law of his members warred against the law of his mind. In agonies he cried, 'Oh, wretched man that I am! Who shall deliver me from this body of death?'"

(The following three paragraphs are from, "The Confessions of Saint Augustine.")

"I was troubled in spirit; most vehemently indignant that I entered not into Thy will and covenant which all my bones cried out unto me to enter, and praised it to the skies. And therein we enter not by ships, or chariots, or feet, no, move not so far as I had come from the house to that place where we were sitting... For not to go only but to go in thither was nothing else but to will resolutely and thoroughly; not to turn and toss, this way and that, a half–divided will.

I cast myself down I know not how, under a certain fig tree giving full vent to my tears; and the floods of mine eyes gushed out an acceptable sacrifice to Thee.

So was I speaking and weeping in the most bitter contrition of my heart when lo! I heard from a neighboring house a boy or girl chanting, "Take up and read." I began to think whether children were wont in any kind of play to sing such words: so checking the torrent of my tears, I arose, interpreting it to be no other than a command from God to open the book, and read the first chapter I should find.

In silence, I read that section on which my eyes first fell: *Not in rioting and drunkenness, not in chambering and wantonness, not in strife and envying; but put ye on the Lord Jesus Christ, and make no provision for the flesh.* No further would I read, nor needed I; for instantly at the end of this sentence, by a light as it were of serenity infused into my heart, all the darkness of doubt vanished away. Too late I loved Thee! … And behold, Thou were within, and I abroad, and there I searched for Thee….Thou were with me, but I was not with Thee…..Thou touched me."

"He was now in the thirty-second year of his age, and resolved to renounce his profession—or, to use his language, "To withdraw from the marts of lip-labor and the selling of words," and enter the service of the new master who had called him to prepare himself for a higher vocation….

Often were discussions with his pupils and friends prolonged into the night and continued until the morning. Plato and Saint Paul 'reappeared' in the garden of Como. Thus three more glorious years were passed in study, in retirement and in profitable discourse, without scandal and without vanity. The proud philosopher was changed into a humble Christian thirsting for a living union with God. The Psalms of David, next to the Epistles of Saint Paul, were his favorite study.

At table, reading and literary conferences were preferred to secular conversation. He was accessible. He interested himself in everybody's troubles, and visited the forlorn and miserable. He was indefatigable in reclaiming those who had strayed from the fold. He won every heart by charity, and captivated every mind with his eloquence; so that Hippo, a little African town was no longer 'least among the cities of Judah.'

It was his mission to head off the dissensions and heresies of his age, and to establish the faith of Paul even among the Germanic barbarians. He is the great theologian of the Church, and his system of divinity not only was the creed of the Middle Ages, but is still an authority in the schools, both Catholic and Protestant.

Augustine showed that purity was an inward virtue; that its passions and appetites are made to be subservient to reason and duty; that the law of temperance is self-restraint.

He thought to be rescued from seductive philosophy and a corrupt life, as he thought, by the special grace of God and in answer to his mother's prayers. He could find no words sufficiently intense whereby to express his gratitude for his deliverance from both sin and error. All his experiences and observations of life confirmed the authority of Scripture, --that the world, as a matter of fact, was sunk in a state of sin and misery, and could be rescued only by that Divine power which converted Paul. It is the helping hand of Omnipotence to the weak will of man,--the weak will even of Paul, when he exclaimed, 'The evil that I would not, that I do….'

No work of man is probably more lasting than, "The Confessions of Augustine." When books were scarce and dear, his various works were the food of Middle Ages. His social and private life had also great charms. He lived the doctrines that he preached… He was affable, courteous, accessible; full of sympathy and kindness. He was tolerant of human infirmities in an age of angry controversy and ascetic rigors. His humility was as marked as his charity, ascribing all his triumphs to Divine assistance."

John Lord, "Beacon Lights of History."

## Thomas a' Kempis

"I will hear what the Lord God speaks within me. Blessed is the soul that hears the Lord speaking within him.

Blessed indeed are those ears that do not listen to the voice which sounds without, but attend to Truth itself teaching within.

Blessed are they that penetrate into those inward things, and by daily exercise strive to make themselves more and more fit for the reception of Heavenly secrets.

Let not Moses, nor any of the Prophets speak to me. Speak Thou rather, O Lord, the Inspirer and Enlightener of all the Prophets; for they alone, without Thee will avail me nothing. They may indeed sound forth words, but they give not the Spirit. Beautifully do they speak; but if Thou be silent, they kindle not the heart. They give the letter, but Thou dost disclose the Spirit. They announce mysteries, but Thou dost unlock their secret meaning. They declare the Commandments, but Thou dost enable us to fulfill them. They work outwardly only, but Thou dost impart understanding.

The glory of a good man is the testimony of a good conscience.

Thou know all things and nothing in a person's conscience is hidden from Thee.

The life of a good religious person ought to excel in all virtues that he may inwardly be such, as outwardly he appears to others.

The Kingdom of God is peace and joy in the Holy Spirit which is not given to the unholy.

If thou had a good conscience, thou would not greatly fear death.

Shut the door of sensual desires that thou may hear what the Lord shall speak in thee.

I daily read two lessons to them: one to rebuke their vices, the other to exhort them to the increase of virtue.

Some have Him in their mouths, but little in their hearts.

There is but little light in us, and that which we have, we quickly lose by our negligence.

Labor now so to live that at the hour of death, thou may rather rejoice than fear.

To Thee I commit myself, and all that is mine, for Thy correction. It is better to be chastised here than hereafter."

Thomas a' Kempis, "The Imitation of Christ," 1441.

## Sebastian Castellio (1515-1563)

"Born 1515 in Eastern France...he became a classical scholar of high rank, and a devoted disciple of the Christ of the Gospels. He wrote a volume of *Sacred Dialogues* out of the Old and New Testaments... This was to be his rubric for life: 'The friend of the truth obeys not the multitude, but the Truth.'

Castellio challenged the words of the Creed: 'He descended into hell.' He felt sure that the words did not rest on any basis of truth, and were to tarnish the Reformation at its birth.

Castellio's emphasis is always on the heart's experience of God. 'Christ asked us to put on the white robes of a pure and holy life, but what occupies our thoughts? We dispute not only over the way to Christ, but over His relation to God the Father; over the Trinity, over predestination, over free will, over the nature of God, of angels and of the condition of the soul after death...Over a multitude of matters that are not essential to salvation, and matters in fact which never can be known until our hearts are pure, for they are things which must be Spiritually perceived.'

He was extremely sensitive to the Divine Voice within his soul. 'I cannot do violence to my conscience,' he cried. 'If I did I should be disobeying Christ. I must be saved or lost by my own personal faith, not by that of another. Christ's doctrine means having a pure heart and a hunger for righteousness.'

After Calvin ordered the burning of Servetus [for denying the Trinity], Castellio wrote, 'I do not defend Servetus. I have never read his books. Calvin burned them together with their author. I do not want to burn Calvin or his book. I am only going to answer it. To burn a man is not to prove a doctrine; it is to burn a man!'

Castellio who called himself 'this poor, humble, peaceable little man.' passed into the peace of God in 1563, and he was borne to his grave on the shoulders of the students of the University of Basle who loved him, and who after his death spread abroad his writings, which bore the seeds of spiritual truth that were to produce a great harvest in their time."

Rufus Jones, "The Luminous Trail."

## George Fox (1624-1691)

"I was born in 1624 in Leicestershire, England. In my very young years I had a gravity and stayedness of mind and spirit not usual in children; insomuch that when I saw old men behave lightly and wantonly towards each other, I had a dislike thereof raised in my heart.

When I came to eleven years of age I knew pureness and righteousness; for while a child I was taught how to walk to be kept pure. The Lord taught me to be faithful in all things, and to act faithfully two ways, viz., inwardly to God, and outwardly, to man...that my words should be few and savory, seasoned with grace; and that I might not eat and drink to make myself wanton, but for health....

As I grew up, my relations thought to have made me a priest; a clergyman, but others persuaded to the contrary. Whereupon I was put to a man who was a shoemaker by trade, and dealt in wool. I never wronged man or woman in all that time; for the Lord's power was with me and over me, to preserve me...When boys and rude persons would laugh at me, I let them alone and went my way; but people had generally a love to me for my innocence and honesty....

Then, at the command of God, the ninth of the seventh month, 1643, I left my relations and broke off all familiarity or fellowship with young or old...As I thus traveled through the country, professors took notice of me, and sought to be acquainted with me; but I was afraid of them, for I was sensible they did not possess what they professed....

During the time I was at Barnet, a strong temptation to despair came upon me. I then saw how Christ was tempted, and mighty troubles I was in. Sometimes I kept myself retired to my chamber, and often walked solitary in the Chase to wait upon the Lord. I wondered why these things should come to me...I thought, because I had forsaken my relations I had done amiss against them.

I was about twenty years of age when these exercises came upon me, and some years I continued in that condition, in great trouble... I went to many a priest to look for comfort, but found no comfort from them….

I returned homeward into Leicestershire, having a regard upon my mind to my parents and relations, lest I should grieve them, for I understood they were troubled at my absence.

Being returned into Leicestershire, my relations would have had me married; but I told them I was but a lad, and must get wisdom.

Then I went to Coventry where I took a chamber for a while at a professor's house till people began to be acquainted with me, for there were many tender people in that town…The priest of Drayton, the town of my birth, came often to me, and another priest sometimes came with him, and they would give place to me to hear me, and I would ask them questions and reason with them. This priest, Stephens, asked me why Christ cried out upon the Cross, "My God, my God, why hast thou forsaken me?" and why He said, "If it be possible, let this cup pass from me; yet not my will, but thine, be done." I told him that at that time the sins of all mankind were upon Him, and their iniquities and transgressions with which He was wounded; which he was to bear, and to be an offering for.

This I spoke, being at that time in a measure sensible of Christ's sufferings….

At that time he would applaud and speak highly of me to others; and what I said in discourse to him on week-days, he would preach of on First-days, which gave me a dislike to him. This priest afterwards became my great persecutor….

When the time called Christmas came, while others were feasting and sporting themselves, I looked out poor widows and gave them some money.

About the beginning of the year 1646, a consideration arose in me how it was said that all Christians are believers, both Protestants and Papists, and the Lord opened to me that if all were believers, then they were all born of God, and passed from death to life, and that none were true believers but such, and though others said they were believers, yet they were not….

I was walking in a field on a First-day morning and the Lord opened unto me that being bred at Oxford or Cambridge was not enough to fit and qualify men to be ministers of Christ, and I wondered at it because it was the common belief of people....

My relations were much troubled that I would not go with them to hear the priest; for I would go into the orchard or the fields, with my Bible, by myself. I asked them, 'Did not the Apostle say to believers that they needed no man to teach them, but as the anointing teaches them?'

When I myself was in the deep, shut up under all, I could not believe that I should ever overcome; my troubles, my sorrows, and my temptations were so great that I thought many times I should have despaired, I was so tempted. While I was in that condition, it was opened unto me by the eternal light and power, and I therein clearly saw that all these troubles were good for me, and temptations for the trial of my faith, which Christ had given me....

I went among the professors at Duckingfield and Manchester, where I stayed awhile, and declared truth among them. There were some convinced who received the Lord's teaching but the professors were in a rage, all pleading for sin and imperfection, and could not endure to hear talk of perfection, and a holy and sinless life. But the Lord's power was over all, though they were chained under darkness and sin, which they pleaded for, and quenched the tender thing in them....

Then came people from far and near to see me; but I was fearful of being drawn out by them; yet I was made to speak, and open things to them.

My sorrows and troubles began to wear off, and tears of joy dropped from me, so that I could have wept night and day with tears of joy to the Lord, in humility and brokenness of heart.

A report went abroad of me that I was a young man that had a discerning spirit; whereupon many came to me from far and near: professors, priests, and people. The Lord's power broke forth, and I had great openings and prophecies, and spoke unto them of the things of God, which they heard with attention and silence, and went away and spread the fame thereof.

George Fox's insights:
He showed me that the priests were out of the true faith, of which Christ is the author,---the faith which purifies, gives victory and brings people to have access to God, by which they please God; the mystery of which faith is held in a pure conscience.

For of all the sects in Christendom so-called that I discoursed with, I found none who could bear to be told that any should come to Adam's perfection,--into that image of God: that righteousness and holiness that Adam was in before he fell, to be clean and pure, without sin, as he was. Therefore how shall they be able to bear being told that any shall grow up to the measure of the stature of the fullness of Christ?

I saw, in that Light and Spirit, which was before the Scriptures were given forth, and which led the holy men of God to give them forth, that all, if they would know God or Christ, or the Scriptures aright, must come to that Spirit by which they that gave them forth were led and taught…As many as should receive Him in His Light, I saw He would give power to become the sons of God which power I had obtained by receiving Christ. I was to direct people to the Spirit that gave forth the Scriptures, by which they might be led into all truth.

In fairs, also and in markets, I was made to declare against their deceitful merchandise, cheating, and cozening; warning all to deal justly, to speak the truth, and to do unto others as they would have others do unto them; forewarning them of the great and terrible day of the Lord which would come upon them all.

I was made to warn masters and mistresses, fathers and mothers in private families, to take care that their children and servants might be trained up in the fear of the Lord, and that themselves should be therein examples and patterns of sobriety and virtue to them.

I told them, 'God dwells not in temples made with hands.' I told them also that all their preaching, baptism and sacrifices would never sanctify them, and bade them look unto Christ within them, and not unto men; for it is Christ that sanctifies. They asked how we knew that Christ did abide in us. I said, 'by His Spirit, that He has given us.'

If you are true believers in Christ you are passed from death to life, and if passed from death then from sin that brings death; and if your faith be true, it will give you victory over sin and the devil; purifying your hearts and consciences. For the true faith is held in a pure conscience, and brings you to please God, and give you access to Him again....

Said I, 'the holy men that wrote the Scriptures pleaded for holiness in heart, life, and conversation here, but since you plead for impurity and sin, which is of the devil; what have you to do with the holy men's words?'

> William Penn's last sentence in his preface to *The Journal*, "Many sons have done virtuously in this day, but dear George, thou excellest them all."
> George Fox, "The Journal of George Fox."

## Jeanne Guyon (1648-1717)

"A lady of true piety and inward devotion came to our house. She had a great esteem for me because I desired to love God. Sometimes she dropped a word to me on the subject of the simplicity of prayer. As my time had not yet come, I did not understand her. Her example instructed me more than her words. I observed in her countenance something which marked a great enjoyment of the presence of God.

At length God permitted a very religious person of the order of St. Francis to pass by my father's dwelling. My father told me what he knew of him, and urged me to go see him. I did not hesitate to speak to him, and tell him in a few words my difficulties about prayer. Presently he replied, 'It is because Madam, you seek *without* what you have *within*. Accustom yourself to seek God in your heart, and you will there find Him.' Having said these words, he left me. They were to me like the stroke of a dart, which penetrated through my heart. These words brought into my heart what I had been seeking so many years. Rather they discovered to me what was there, and which I had not enjoyed for want of knowing it. ...It was for want of understanding these words of Thy Gospel, "The Kingdom of God comes not with observation. The Kingdom of God is within you." This I now experienced... He had given me an experience of His presence in my soul; not by thought or any application of mind but as a thing really possessed after the sweetest manner.

By means of charity, the two other virtues of faith and hope are introduced. Faith so strongly seizes on the understanding, as to make it decline all reasoning... By means of the will and love, all are reunited in the center of the soul in God who is our ultimate end. According to St. John, 'He who dwells in love, dwells in God for God is Love.'

As He never ceases to speak, so He never ceases to operate. If people once came to know the operations of the Lord in souls wholly resigned to His guiding, it would fill them with reverential admiration and awe.

One day as I walked to church, followed by a footman, I was met by a poor man. I went to give him alms; he thanked me but refused them, and then spoke to me in a wonderful manner of God and of divine things. He displayed to me my whole heart, my love to God, my charity, my too great fondness for my beauty and all my faults. He told me it was not enough to avoid hell, but that the Lord required of me the utmost purity and height of perfection. My heart assented to his reproofs. I heard him with silence and respect; his words penetrated my very soul... I never saw him again.

Though He leaves us for a time to prove and exercise our faith, yet He never fails us when our need of Him is the more pressing.

The impure and selfish soul is hereby purified as gold in the furnace; full of its own judgment and its own will before, but now obeys like a child and finds no other will in itself... Before it preferred itself above everybody; now everybody above itself; having a boundless charity for its neighbor, to bear with his faults and weaknesses in order to win him by love.

If we walk uprightly He will never fail us. He would sooner do miracles for us. He showed me that it is not the actions in themselves which please Him, but the constant ready obedience to every discovery of His will, even in the minutest things."

"Madame Guyon"<br>
*Autobiography*

# BIBLIOGRAPHY

The Bible, King James Version; Emphasis on The New Testament.

Adam, Karl "The Spirit of Catholicism," 1924. (R.Q).

Augustine, Aurelius, (Saint) (354-430) "The Confessions of Saint Augustine." Random House Inc. 1949.

Aurelius, Marcus, (161-180 A.D, reign) "Meditations" by Walter J. Black Inc. 1945.

Bamfield, K.B. "On Values," 1922. (R.Q).

Barclay, Robert, "An Apology for the True Christian Divinity of the People called Quakers," 1675. Friends' Book Store, 1906.

Bonhoeffer, Dietrich, "The Cost of Discipleship," The Macmillan Company, 1963.

Coleridge, Samuel T., (1772-1834) "The Works of Samuel Taylor Coleridge." Black's Readers service. Roslyn, New York, 1950.

_____ "Aids to Reflections" Cosimo Classics, New York, 2005.

de Tocqueville, Alexis, "Democracy in America," 1835 New American Library, ed. by Richard D. Heffner, 1956.

Dhammapada c. 5th C. B.C. (R.Q).

Emerson, Ralph Waldo, "Selected Essays, Lectures and Poems:" *Divinity School Address*, July 15, 1838. Simon & Schuster, New York, 1965.

Fenelon, Francois, (1651-1715), "Spiritual Letters." (R.Q.)

Forrester, W.R., "Christian Vocation," 1951. (R.Q.)

Fox, George, (1624-1691) "The Journal of George Fox," Capricorn Books, New York, 1963.

Franklin, Benjamin, (1706-1790): "The Completed Autobiography of Benjamin Franklin." Regenery Publcations, Lanham, Md., 2006.

Galileo, Galilei, "Dialogue on the Great World Systems."1632 (R.Q)

Guyon, Jeanne, (1648-1717) "Madame Guyon," *Autobiography*, Moody Press.

Harith IBN Asad al-Muhasibi c. 850 A.D., (R.Q).

Jones, Rufus, "The Luminous Trail." The Macmillan Company, New York, 1947.

Kingsland, William, "Our Infinite Life," 1922, (R.Q)

Kempis, Thomas a' "The Imitation of Christ" (1441). A Mentor-Omega Book: The New American Library of World Literature, Inc. New York, 1962.

Law, William, "Christian Perfection," 1726. (R.Q).

Lord, John "Beacon Lights of History," Vol. 1: "*Seeking After Truth*"; "Abraham" Wm H. Wise, Co., New York, 1888.

\_\_\_\_\_ *Antiquity: Saint Augustine*. Fords, Howard and Hulbert, New York, 1883.

Luther, Martin, (1483-1546) "On Romans chapter 6," *Martin Luther*, by John Dillenburger, N.Y.

Mercier, D.J., *Conferences of,* 1907. (R. Q).

Milton, John, (1608-1674) "Paradise Lost," (1667) The Odyssey Press: New York, 1962.

_____Poems Selected by Laurence Lerner, *Penguin Books, 1953.*

Nahman, Rabbi of Bratslav: (1772-1811): "Quoted in *Judaism*... 1961" (R.Q).

Paine, Thomas, "The Age of Reason" 1794, Barnes & Noble Inc., New York, 2006.

Pascal, Blaise, "Pensees," (1670), translated by A. J. Krailsheimer. Penguin Books, 1995.

Plato, "De Legibus, Lib. X1," 4<sup>th</sup> C. B.C. (R.Q)

Redford, R. A., "Vox Dei" (*Doctrine of the Spirit*). Curts and Jennings, Cincinnati, 1889.

Socrates....(470-399 B. C), "Trial and Death of Socrates," *The Apology of Socrates* from *The Dialogues of Plato,* Translated by F.J. Church, A.L. Burt, Co. New York.

Stott, John R. W., "Basic Christianity," Inter-Varsity Press, London, 1971.

Wesley, Reverend John, "Wesleyan Theology," *Sermons.* Lane & Scott: New York, 1850.

Whittier, John G., "The Complete Poetical Works of John Greenleaf Whittier," The Riverside Press, Cambridge, 1894.

*Woods, Ralph L., (compiled and edited): "The World Treasury of Religious Quotations," Garland Books, New York, 1966.

*The Initials, 'R. Q' ("Religious Quotations") noted with various works, refer to Ralph Wood's book as the source of those quotation.

Made in the USA
Monee, IL
02 March 2022